Disinformation: Identifying Devious Data and Iffy Information

Paul Finlay

Relativistic

Relativistic Books

Copyright C 2018 Paul Finlay
All rights reserved.

First published in Great Britain by Relativistic

Unless permitted under UK copyright law, this work may only be reproduced, in any written, printed or electronic form with prior permission of the publisher.

ISBN-10: 978-1-9993253-0-5

THANKS

To three groups of people. First, my assiduous proof readers, Ann, Mike, Steve and Susie who have improved this book immeasurably, with additional thanks to Steve for helping with publication. Second, John Hudson and John Sarginson and my colleagues at The Friary, West Bridgford who have donated their copies of The Daily Mail, The Daily Telegraph, The Times and several other newspapers over many months. And third, Mike Collett and Becky Russell who have helped me in the production of the diagrams, and Malcolm Hill and Ian Young for their incisive observations on the book's contents.

CONTENTS

Foreword	vii
Introduction	1
Chapter 1 Summarising Datasets	4
Chapter 2 What's Being Reported?	13
Chapter 3 Sampling	24
Chapter 4 Statistics about Populations	33
Chapter 5 Association, Regression, Correlation and Causation	45
Chapter 6 Forecasting and Scenarios	55
Chapter 7 How do Things Compare?	64
Chapter 8 How are Things Progressing?	75
Chapter 9 The Commentariat and its Data Sources	87
Glossary	104
Endnotes	110

FOREWORD

In the 2016 EU Referendum the choice for UK voters was either to *Remain* in the European Union or to *Leave* it (Brexit). The position regarding people with relevant experience and expertise was that:

- All living Prime Ministers wanted Remain
- All living Chancellors (except Nigel Lawson) wanted Remain
- All living Foreign Secretaries wanted Remain
- The vast majority of MPs in Parliament wanted Remain
- All political parties in the UK (except UKIP and a fringe Northern Irish party) had Remain as their policy – Conservative, Labour, Liberal Democrats, Greens, SNP, the Welsh Nationalist and most Northern Irish parties
- Overwhelmingly, both national and international economists stated their belief that Brexit would adversely affect the UK economy

With this backing for Remain the UK voted to Leave !

During the 2016 US Presidential election campaign Donald Trump popularized the term 'fake news'. Of course he was using the term about other people's news – which is ironic as he is almost certainly the biggest source of fake news in US political history. Whilst all politicians distort to some extent, Trump's way of campaigning went far beyond anything that had been seen before, seemingly with little or no concern for the truth.

Many commentators saw the outcomes of these two campaigns as reinforcing the view that data and logic never won elections: what won the day were such things as an ability to address people's feelings and tap into their emotions. Broad political values and the character of politicians were much more important than detailed policies. One leading light[1] in the Brexit referendum campaign who, it should be noted, had been the UK Secretary of State for Education, even went so far as to say that the UK electorate were fed up with experts – and he endorsed this rejection of expertise!

The indications are that the lack of attention to facts doesn't appear to have changed since these two campaigns. After the Brexit vote the UK Department for Exiting the EU produced a set of Economic Impact Assessments. Only 83 parliamentarians out of the 1,450 MPs and peers bothered to look at them[2]. This suggests minds had already been made up – any new facts were irrelevant. Hans Rosling in his best-selling book Factfulness[3] provides numerous examples from the field of world health where specialists were extremely ignorant of the contexts within which their expertise was being used. The Washington Post[4] reported in August 2018 that Trump had made over 4,000 false or misleading claims since his inauguration in January 2017.

The term 'fake news' is now almost meaningless as it's often used simply to dismiss any news that's found disagreeable. A better term is disinformation – information intended to deceive or mislead. It's very important to make a distinction between two forms of disinformation – between lies and misleading statements. [This is the distinction made in the EU code of practice on disinformation][5]. Lies are downright falsehoods such as when Trump insisted that the crowd at his inauguration was the biggest ever for such an event, and when he boasted[6] that he had told Canadian Prime Minister Justin Trudeau that the U.S. had a trade deficit with Canada despite admitting having "no idea" if that was true. In the run up to Brexit the claim was made[7] that Turkey would be joining the EU by 2020 and the UK could do nothing to stop it. These were downright lies made openly by public figures. Many, many more lies are propagated anonymously on social media and such fabrications aren't the sort of thing that ordinary people with limited investigative time could be expected to unearth. Fortunately, there are now organisations[8] that are carrying out fact checking and calling out downright lies. These organisations are moving to provide computer systems that will allow for real-time fact checking – commenting on a politician's speech as it unfolds for example.

Misleading statements are different to lies. They aren't outright falsehoods but arise when someone is being devious, when they are being 'economical with the truth'. Generally, misleading statements have less individual impact than downright lies but they are more insidious and their sheer number means it's impossible for the fact checkers to challenge all but a few of them. These features mean that the reader/viewer is generally on their own when sifting or discounting misleading claims.

The prevalence of devious advocacy and the valuing of emotion over facts hasn't gone unnoticed. Two significant reports were published in the UK in the early part of 2018. A House of Lords report[9] called for children and adults to be educated to allow them to identify misleading information online. The House of Commons all-party parliamentary group on literacy[10] called for teachers to be provided with training resources to help children navigate news stories.

This book is part of the fight against devious advocacy and misinformation. It's concerned with making the reader aware when tricks are being used and thus be better able to judge the validity of news items. Whilst many examples in the book are from politics, the lessons are applicable to any decision making process, particularly those where numbers are involved.

The people who are likely to appreciate this book are those who aren't versed in data analysis but who would like to be able to more readily interpret the data that's used to advocate particular courses of action. However, it's not only the consumers of information who need to be vigilant. In a world full of instant and often untrustworthy social media it's vital that the standards of the main-stream media can be relied on. Thus another important audience for this book are journalists and other media commentators.

Grandiose as it may sound I can do no better than to quote the watchword of The Washington Post – **Democracy Dies in Darkness**. I hope this book will increase the illumination.

November 2018

INTRODUCTION

This book has been written to help people become more aware of how commentators in the media select pieces of data and weave them into news stories. Its focus is on devious advocacy. Before getting into this topic however, there are two interlinked concepts that it's valuable to consider. These are the concepts of population/sample and descriptive/inferential statistics. A bit boring perhaps, but it takes only a couple of pages.

Suppose for some reason there's a need to measure the heights of all 30 students in a class of year 6 school children. These children together constitute a set and the 30 pieces of height data would be termed a dataset. We can characterize this set in many ways: we can calculate the average height, the maximum height, the range of heights, how many children are less than a certain height and so on. Each of these pieces of data is a statistic that can be used to describe aspects of the dataset. They are descriptive statistics.

Here we have a class of 30 children and only 30 children: we aren't considering any other children or classes. For all intents and purposes this class is our world and the children in it are the population of this world. We have considered the whole population and our statistics describe this population.

Suppose now that there's a requirement to get country-wide data on the heights of year 6 children. Now the population of concern is all the nation's year 6 children. We could go ahead and measure all the children in this population, create a dataset and produce descriptive statistics from it.

But what if it's simply too expensive to measure all the children? In this case the best we could do is to measure some of the children and then infer from this data what the statistics for the nation's children are likely to be. The 'some of the children' is a sample of the population of children and we would be moving from the descriptive statistics found for this sample to infer the statistics for the whole population. We move from descriptive statistics to inferential statistics. If the sample is chosen well and it's large, then the sample statistics are likely to be a good guide to the population statistics. If say, the average height of the children in the sample was 140cms, then we would expect the average height in the population to be close to 140cms - perhaps lying between 139 and 141cms. We shouldn't expect that the average height of the nation's year 6 children to be exactly 140cms, although 140cms is the best estimate we can make.

Note that the term population isn't restricted to describing a group of people – it's a general term used for any collection of things – the population of cars say, or the population of laptop computers. Items within a population are termed individuals and thus we have individual cars and individual laptops. The things we want to know about the individuals and the population as a whole are termed attributes. Many attributes are variables (height, voting habits, fuel consumption, failure rates) that can take on different values.

Key terminology The term *population* refers to all the people/things about which we are interested: a *sample* is a subset of the population. The sample will contain *individuals* whose measured *attributes* will provide a *dataset*. If data for a whole population is obtained, the statistics developed are *descriptive statistics* and there's no need to infer anything about the population – all is known. If the population is sampled rather than all individuals being measured, then we have descriptive statistics for the sample and we need to use the tools of *inferential statistics* to infer the most appropriate values to characterize the population.

The structure of the book The book consists of 4 sets of chapters. The book opens with two chapters that are concerned with descriptive statistics – characterisations of a fully-defined dataset. Averages and measures of spread are explored in the first chapter: boring possibly but quite instructive, and it leads on to an interesting discussion in Chapter 2 of the ways in which measures are clouded through the use of such things as inflation and surrogates.

In Chapters 3 and 4 we consider inferential statistics, beginning by exploring what makes a good sample and then discussing how confident we can be in our inferences about the population from which the sample has been taken. Because some readers might find chapter 4 a difficult read, an expanded list of key points has been provided. Thus if you do find chapter 4 hard going I suggest that you simply jump to these key points.

In these first 4 chapters the concern is with one factor or variable – voting intentions or children's heights for example. Often, of course, one variable is related to others and these relationships are considered in the next two chapters. In chapter 5 we discuss correlation and association and consider the thorny question of cause and effect. In Chapter 6 the roles of modelling, big data and predictive analytics are discussed and forecasting and scenarios are explored.

Attempting to judge something against an ideal is generally unhelpful: there's almost always a need to compare with other situations to understand the significance of new information. In chapter 7 the evaluations are with other comparable areas – geographical, social, political and economic – attempting to answer the question *How do things compare?* Chapter 8 considers another form of context – across time and with how things are changing – attempting to answer the question *How are things progressing?*

In Chapter 9 we look at the context in which news items are produced and presented to us. The validity of the data sources are examined, the professional commentators themselves are assessed and the media outlets they use are evaluated.

1 SUMMARISING DATASETS

> **Beware the selective use of summary statistics** Once a dataset is larger than a few items it needs to be summarised if its pertinent features are to be shared. Overwhelmingly, the summary will consist of an average of the values together with a measure of how much the values differ amongst each other. There are several measures that can be used for each of these important statistics and the ones chosen are likely to be those that best support the advocate's position. Thus always try to identify which forms of average and spread are being used and ask the questions: Why has this particular measure been chosen? What if a different measure had been selected?

Before the 2015 UK election the Labour Party leader Ed Miliband made the following claim[1]: *People are £1,600 a year worse off than they were when the coalition government came to power.* Presumably he was talking about an average – but which one?

Imagine that you work in a 20-person business. Your boss calls you in and gives you a pay rise, telling you that you now earn above the company average. This makes you feel good, but do you know what the boss means by 'above the company average'?

Disinformation: identifying devious data and iffy information

The 20 values in table 1.1 comprise the dataset of the annual salaries of you and your colleagues. If you wanted to communicate to someone all the information that could be extracted from this dataset then you would have to provide all these data points – quite a long-winded process even with just 20 pieces of data. To do so with the volumes of data generated every day on all manner of things becomes impossible. Thus there's a need to summarise the dataset - characterize it using only a few (normally one or two) 'encapsulating' values.

Table 1.1 Annual salaries (£)

20,104	30,428	40,432	53,216
20,339	35,752	42,876	53,538
21,000	36,091	43,456	55,285
21,246	37,278	46,744	56,375
24,313	38,429	52,368	58,210

What's the meaning of 'average'? One obvious thing you would like to have in any summary is the value around which the data points tend to cluster – the average. You will almost certainly be thinking that an average salary would always be calculated by simply adding up all the salaries and dividing the total by the number of employees. For your company this average comes to just over £39,000. As you earn £40,432 you are happy to hear this - that you are indeed earning 'above the company average'.

So far so good. But if you stop to reflect on what this average tells you, you will see that it tells you very little. Yes, you know how it has been calculated and that your salary is above the average but where are you in relation to other people? How many of your colleagues earn more than you? What happens to the average if a new post is created that pays £200,000 per year? Well, the average changes to over £47,000 and so then your salary will be below the average – and well below the average. Are you similar to other people or are you an outlier?

Adding together all the values in a dataset and dividing by the number of items in the set produces an average that's called the mean[2]. However, there are alternate measures of central tendency that can be more useful in certain circumstances. Here we meet a common problem where professional usage of a term isn't the same as common usage. For professionals, the term average can be applied to several measures of central tendency, whereas the layperson almost always thinks of the mean when an average is mentioned. This distinction between expert and the ordinary usage is obviously one that can be exploited by the skilled advocate.

Scales of measurement Only 3 averages are in widespread use and we need to look at a bit of theory to understand where they could be used appropriately: we need now to consider *scales of measurement*.

Sometimes all we can do with a set of items is to differentiate between them – we make no other distinction. A typical case where we might use numbers simply to make a distinction is in personal information, with perhaps 1 = single, 2 = married, 3 = widowed, 4 = divorced etc. There's no implication of 'goodness' or 'size' or any other attribute in the assigned numbers. These measurements are being made on a nominal scale of measurement – numbers are simply names.

A scale of measurement recording more information is the ordinal scale, which measures individuals according to the magnitude of something about them: the higher the number assigned the more of the attribute the individual possesses. A common use of ordinal scales is in questionnaire/opinion polls. Typically, you might be asked to score a service on the scale 1 = poor, 2 = adequate, 3 = good, 4 = very good, 5 = excellent. The greater the number assigned the better the service. Note that it would be wrong to think that a score of 3 is 2 units of anything meaningfully higher that a score of 1: good is better than poor but it can't be said that it's 2 units better or 3 times as good. Whilst you can't sensibly calculate a mean when you are using an ordinal scale of measurement, you can see the temptation to calculate it anyway when discussing the results from (ordinally measured) opinion polls – a temptation often not resisted. The results from doing this aren't very meaningful.

A ratio scale is needed to signify the amount of something. What's required is that equal differences between amounts of something are reflected in equal differences in their measurements, and that zero signifies a complete lack of the attribute. Typical variables that are measured on a ratio scale are the many accounting measures – profit, turnover, debt. A difference between £20 and £30 is the same as the difference between £200 and £210; £40 is twice £20; £400 is twice £200.

So
nominal = naming
ordinal = naming and ordering
ratio = naming, ordering and sizing

A contributor to a *More or Less* radio programme[3] on the perils of swimming in open waters explained that we're used to swimming in swimming pools where the temperature is 30°C, whereas sea, river and reservoir waters are typically less than 15°C. He then went on to say *that's at least half the temperature.* You can readily see that this is nonsensical if you consider that the same information could be given using the Fahrenheit scale (59°F and 86°F) or the Kelvin scale (288°K and 303°K). You wouldn't be tempted to say that one temperature is half the other with these two scales – but the hotness/coldness of the waters remains the same. The error occurs because the contributor is using an inappropriate scale, considering Celsius to be a ratio scale when it's ordinal. [Zero on the Celsius scale doesn't correspond to an absence of heat, it's simply a convenient point on the scale].

Three measures of the average

The mean To sensibly calculate a mean requires that we have used a ratio scale to collect the data in the dataset. This is the case for the salary data listed in table 1.1. Given that the mean carries so little information you may well ask why this average is used so frequently. Well, for one thing it's easy to calculate. More substantial answers are that the mean uses all the data in the dataset and that statisticians can do manipulations with it that produce very useful insights. Note that the value of the mean may not be one that exists within the dataset. For example, the mean for 4 people earning £20,000, £30,000, £40,000 and £50,000 is £35,000.

The median Calculation of the median requires the dataset to be acquired using an ordinal or ratio scale. If all the data points are placed in order, the median is the 'value in the middle'. The median value splits the

Chapter 1 Summarising datasets

number of values into two equal parts, 50% on one side and 50% on the other. In the company dataset the median is just over £38,000. As with the mean, the value of the median may not exist in the dataset.

One advantage of using the median – with 50% of measurements below and 50% above the median value – is that it's an average that isn't affected much by extreme values. This downplaying of any extremes is valuable when the distribution is skewed or when it seems reasonable to reduce the importance of outliers - perhaps because they may be suspected of being measured incorrectly. Common measures of poverty are related to the threshold of 60% of the median household income; the threshold is linked to the median so that a few very high earners don't skew the cut-off level.

Tricky means and medians The initial annual salaries of the 9 lowest paid company employees[4], rounded to the nearest £'000, are set out as row A in table 1.2.

Table 1.2 Tricky means and medians – lowest salaries £'000 pa.											Mean	Median
A			20	20	21	21	24	30	36	36	37	27.1	24
B			22	22	23	23	26	32	37	38	39	29.1	26
C	18	18	22	22	23	23	26	32	37	38	39	27.1	23

Suppose that everyone is given a £2,000 pay rise. Naturally both the mean and median rise by £2,000 (row B). Suppose again that this pay rise is followed by the recruitment of two trainees each paid £18,000 pa (row C). Compared to the position before the pay rise the company mean has remained the same but the median has dropped by £1,000. Compared with the situation after the pay rise the mean has dropped by £2,000 and the median by £3,000. This drop in the median salary certainly looks bad. But all the original employees have had a salary increase of £2,000 and two trainees have found jobs. Everybody in the company is no doubt happy with this state of affairs, but you can see how in certain circumstances the change in the median salary can be used to good effect by politicians. This was presumably why Ed Miliband used the median rather than the mean.

The mode The mode is the value that occurs most frequently in the dataset. As with the median one valuable thing is that it doesn't change

Disinformation: identifying devious data and iffy information

much if there's an extreme value in the dataset: by definition one extreme value won't alter the mode at all as it's unique and won't become the most frequent. The mode may be the best average to use when a substantial proportion of the observations take the same value.

Figure 1.1

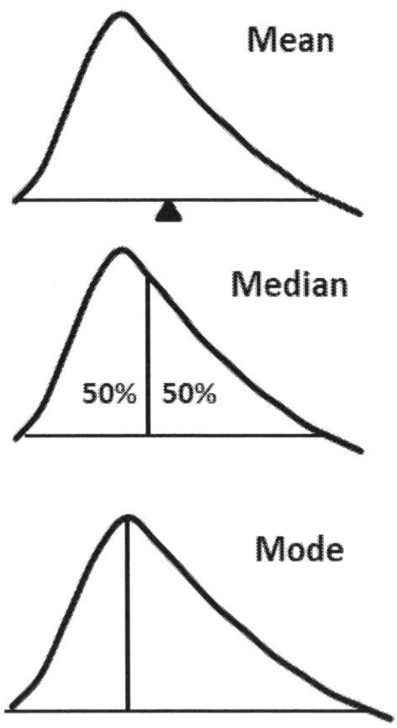

Mean

Median

50% | 50%

Mode

Figure 1.1 shows graphically the differences for these 3 averages. The little triangle under the first graph represents a fulcrum – illustrating that the mean is like a seesaw with equal 'weights' on either side.

Table 1.3 gives a numerical comparison using a dataset of 7 values. This dataset is used here instead of that in table 1.1 because with the company dataset it isn't possible to state what the value of the mode is. The reason for this lies in something we haven't looked at yet - the difference between discrete and continuous data.

A company salary could be any value between, say, £20,000 and £200,000. Because it can take on any value in this range

Table 1.3 Comparison of 'averages' of the values 1, 2, 2, 3, 3, 4, 5

Type	Description	Example	Result
Mean	Sum of the values in the dataset divided by the number of values	(1+2+2+3+3+4+5) / 7	2.86
Median	Middle value of the dataset	1, 2, 2, 3, 3, 4, 5	3
Mode	Most frequent value in the dataset	1, 2, 2, 3, 3, 4, 5	2 3

it is a continuous variable. It's very likely that each salary is a unique or almost unique value and so to identify a value as the most frequently occurring is generally impossible and always senseless. Contrast this with opinion poll values which only take on values such as 1, 2, 3, 4, 5….. These values are discrete and an opinion poll dataset is composed of discrete variables. With discrete variables we <u>can</u> identify the mode – the most frequent value.

Measures of spread

So far we have considered how to summarise the central tendency that occurs in a dataset. We used the company salary dataset in table 1.1 to illustrate the statistics used. The dataset shown in table 1.4 is the data for salaries in a similar small company. These two datasets have the same calculable averages – the means are identical and the medians are sensibly the same. But the values in the datasets are distributed very differently. We need a measure of this distribution – a measure of 'how far from the middle' the values lie. There are 4 measures of spread in common use: the range, the interquartile range, the standard deviation and the variance.

Table 1.4 Annual salaries (£)

19,000	28,560	38,760	55,420
19,500	34,477	40,000	56,706
19,700	35,205	44,600	58,034
21,200	36,300	47,803	61,000
22,074	38,217	47,990	62,700

The range The simplest and the most intuitive way to characterise the spread of the data points is simply to calculate the difference between the maximum and minimum values. This can be useful if you are measuring a variable that has either a critical high or low threshold that shouldn't be crossed. The range will instantly inform you whether at least one value has broken a threshold. Whilst this can be useful in a few cases, it's a very poor way of summarising the whole of the distribution and isn't widely used.

The interquartile range This measure can most easily be thought of as the 'middle half' of the observed values. Formally it's defined as the difference between the lower and upper quartiles ie., the values that are respectively one quarter and three-quarters of the way along the ranked set of observations. For this reason, the interquartile range is often reported along with the median as the best choice to capture the spread and average when dealing with skewed data and data with suspect outliers. It avoids any distortion from extremely high or low values and it can also be estimated 'by eye' from graphs. Its general disadvantage is that it ignores one half of

Disinformation: identifying devious data and iffy information

the values completely.

The interquartile range is the most commonly-used 'range' statistic but it's perfectly possible to use any portions of the distribution of data values for comparison purposes; for example, the lowest 20% (the lowest quintile) could be used and contrasted with the top 20% (the highest quintile). You can imagine how the selection of the percentage for comparison can be used in advocacy.

Variance and standard deviation For any measure of spread we would like to use all the data points in the dataset. The most obvious way to do this is simply to calculate the average, calculate the distance away from this average (the deviation) for every data point and then calculate the average of these deviations. However, this will produce both positive and negative deviations – cancelling or almost cancelling each other out. Obviously one could ignore the sign of the negative values and get a measure that sums up the spread quite well. The spread calculated in this way is termed the absolute average deviation – absolute because the signs of the deviations are ignored.

For technical reasons that we shan't concern ourselves with here, statisticians don't often use the absolute average deviation but instead make use of the squares of the differences of the data values from the mean of the dataset. They multiply each difference by itself, and since two negative numbers multiplied together produce a positive number, this gets over the problem of cancellation that occurs with average deviations. All the squared values are then added up and their mean is calculated. This mean squared deviation is termed the variance. The variance, whilst extremely useful to statisticians, isn't very useful to the layperson as the units are unhelpful: it isn't very useful to talk about a mean salary of £39,000pa and a spread (variance) of £25,000 squared pounds. The way round it is to take the square root of the variance and use that. The square root is the value that when multiplied by itself gives the original value. Thus the square root of 25 (denoted by $\sqrt{25}$) is 5, since 5 x 5 = 25). The square root of the variance is called the standard deviation. We will see the use of the standard deviation in later chapters – particularly Chapter 4.

Chapter 1 Summarising datasets

The most useful summary statistics[5] for the datasets in tables 1.1 and 1.4 are set out in table 1.5.

Table 1.5 Summary of the main measures for the two datasets (£'000)							
	Mean	Median	Mode	Range	Interquartile range	Quintile	Standard Deviation
Table 1.1	39,365	38,430	N/A	40,106	28,903	33,112	13,028
Table 1.4	39,365	38,762	N/A	43,700	33,346	35,506	14,295

Key points
- The choice of the statistics to use when categorising a dataset can significantly alter the messages that are being presented.
- There are 3 averages in common use – the mean, the median and the mode. The mean shouldn't be used when the data is ranked data, as is normally the case from questionnaires and polls. The mode can only be used with discrete data.
- There are several measures of spread in common use – the range, the standard deviation, the interquartile range and sundry other '-iles'. The standard deviation is the most commonly-used measure of spread.

2 WHAT'S BEING REPORTED?

> **Know what the data refers to** When you read a news story are you sure you know what the author is describing? This isn't a question about whether the data is being used appropriately or not, simply what the data refers to. One way to get a grip on this is to ask simple questions of the news item such as what exactly is the subject of the article and do the financial figures include inflation or not. Only by being sure of the answers to questions such as these can you be reasonably sure you know what's being discussed and identify any deceptions that may be occurring.

When confronted by a news item the first thing to consider is the relationship between its author, funding bodies and the host news channel. An item on climate change from an oil-funded think tank should be scrutinised very differently from a weather report on Gardeners' World. Such scrutiny is so important that it's been given a chapter all on its own (Chapter 9): in this chapter we won't be challenging the background of a news item, only concentrating on identifying what is being reported on.

Three simple questions should always be asked about a news item: who/what is being reported on, what are the time periods being discussed and which geographical areas are being considered. And running through all of this is to ask how appropriate are any comparisons that are being made. Financial reporting poses its own problems.

Chapter 2 What's being reported?

Three Very Basic Questions

Who/what is being reported on? The previous chapter opened with the statement by Ed Milliband[1] *People are £1,600 a year worse off than they were when the coalition government came to power.* This claim may well be true, but what did Ed Miliband mean by 'people'? In fact he was excluding about half the adult population: he was excluding pensioners, benefit recipients, part-time workers and the self-employed. He meant only full-time employees and only their earnings before taxes and benefits. 'Who is being reported on?' is a very special group whose composition is well concealed. The statement does seem to be putting the best possible slant on the available data.

Another aspect of who/what? is the use of surrogate measures. In many policy areas it's difficult to measure what you want to measure. Poverty is one such difficult area. In 1995 the United Nations[2] adopted two definitions of poverty. *Absolute poverty* was defined as a condition characterised by severe deprivation of basic human needs, including food, safe drinking water, sanitation facilities, health, shelter, education and information. There was also *overall poverty* that includes a lack of income and productive resources to ensure sustainable livelihoods.

In developed countries it's *relative poverty* that's of political concern. The main relative poverty measure[3] used by the OECD and the EU is based on "economic distance". Here the poverty rate is taken as the proportion of the people in a given age group whose income falls below half the median household income of the total population. In the UK[4] two measures of poverty have been used for several years, both linked to 60% of the median income of the population as a whole. People considered to live in *relative poverty* have their household income compared to the average median income in the current year. Those who are considered to live in *absolute poverty* have their household income compared to the median income in the 'anchor year' of 2010 (when the coalition government took office). [This measure was introduced as relative poverty had the disadvantage that it would remain unchanged if everyone gained as the overall economy prospered: this is not the case with absolute poverty]. Both rates could be reported including or excluding housing costs.

Disinformation: identifying devious data and iffy information

The Joseph Rowntree Foundation[5] uses the simple word *poverty* where others use the phrase relative poverty and has a further definition – *persistent poverty* - defined as being currently in poverty and having been so for at least two out of the previous 3 years. The second Cameron administration came under attack for its redefinition of poverty; poverty was no longer to be classified by family income but whether a family was in work or not. The associated measures were *relative low income* and *absolute low income*. The UK government also has a definition of *deprivation* - the entitlement of children to free school meals.

In 2018 two new approaches to defining poverty were developed in the UK, both aiming to move away from simply looking at income as an indicator of poverty. The Legatum Institute[6] looked at total household resources and recognised that factors other than income may put people into poverty or pull them out of it, such as whether a household contains someone with a disability, whether there are childcare costs and whether there are personal savings. The Institute's poverty line is 55% of the average median income over the last 3 years - a half-way position between the years that had been used previously to calculate relative and absolute poverty. It defined households which had spent the majority of the past 4 years below the poverty line as being in *persistent poverty*.

The second approach provides a new characterisation of *disadvantage*[7]. Here a *no-frills standard of living* has been identified through a consensus of ordinary citizens. This calls for an income that allows people to participate in a recognised range of social and cultural activities – such as taking an annual holiday and paying for such things as swimming lessons and the costs of belonging to the scouts/guides. And finally, we have a columnist[8] writing about Greece …and that the numbers *at risk of poverty* have risen by eight percentage points…

So here we have 10 terms and measures used when referring to poverty - *absolute poverty, overall poverty, relative poverty, persistent poverty, relative low income, absolute low income, deprivation, disadvantage, no-frills standard of living,* and *at risk of poverty* – and with different definitions for the same term in some cases. Lots of potential for confusion and dissembling here.

Chapter 2 What's being reported?

Which time periods are being considered? It's common, especially in radio and TV news bulletins, to hear numbers quoted but without clearly stated associated time periods. At the 2017 Conservative Party Conference[9] the Chancellor Philip Hammond announced £400million of extra money for Northern Transport. This turns out to be money either already announced or not due to be spent until after 2020. Additionally, the Chancellor announced £20billion extra funding for the NHS by 2020 – does this mean the cumulative amount over the period up to 2020, up to and including 2020, or a sum given every year increasing to £20billion in 2020? To make sense of such announcements it's very important to always be clear on the choice of time periods, stated or not. When making comparisons it may be reasonable to choose the start and end dates of a government or the start and end of a decade, but if more arbitrary dates are chosen the reason is likely to be a devious one.

In mid-September 2017 the UK government announced that it was going to lift the wage cap for the police with a mean pay rise of 2%. Critics didn't think this adequately addressed the issue of police pay. Theresa May's defence of the pay policy was robust. She stated in the House of Commons that an officer who joined the Police Service in 2010 had had a pay rise of around 32% in real terms, so the 2% now was quite a generous settlement.

Why had Mrs May chosen 2010 as her base level for comparison? And why pick on the recruits of that year? There were two good reasons – it was the year when the coalition government took office and also when she became Home Secretary. It was also a perfect date for Mrs May as new recruits in that year had special treatment. The Radio 4 programme[10] *More or Less* further analysed the 32% claim with the points listed in textbox 2.1.

Mrs May was correct in the sense that her figures were correct, but of course she wasn't answering the main criticism. *More or Less* went on to say that only 4% of police officers joined the Police Service in 2010 and not all of those got the 32% pay rise. So in her statement Mrs May was both very selective in who she was reporting on and very selective in her choice of comparison dates. Police Federation analysis of Home Office figures showed that a police constable had a mean pay rise over this period of £517, which is a 16% reduction in real terms.

[It's interesting to note that Mrs May's 32% included the effect of an increase in the amount of income that's not taxed – the personal allowance. So, when there's another hike in this allowance expect your boss to tell you that you have had a pay increase!]

Textbox 2.1 Rise in Police Pay

Police recruits joining in 2010:
- were the last to join before the 2-year public sector pay freeze in 2011
- joined before the pay reforms of 2013 which changed the increment pay scales
- joined before the Chancellor started to raise the personal allowance

Also it turned out that:
- during the pay freeze most police officers had their pay increments frozen but this did not apply to those on the 3 lowest scales, so new officers got incremental pay rises
- the recruits joined just before new pay scales were introduced and some new joiners moved up the pay scales more quickly than colleagues who joined before 2010
- in 2010 the personal allowance was £6,475: in 2017 it was £11,500

Which geographical areas are being considered? You hear that the unemployment rate is 5%: is this for the whole of the UK, for England, for the West Midlands, for Birmingham? One particular confusion arises over the loose use of the terms Great Britain, the UK and sometimes even the British Isles[11]. The UK is the United Kingdom of Great Britain and Northern Ireland, with Great Britain being England, Scotland and Wales. Further confusion occurs as colloquially the terms UK, Britain and Great Britain are used interchangeably (another example of usage where the expert uses words differently from the ordinary person). As can be imagined, the confusion can be much worse when the EU or other

Chapter 2 What's being reported?

geographical groupings are being referenced. Very many people confuse the European Court of Human Rights – which is a Europe-wide body involving 47 member states and based in Strasbourg - with the European Court of Justice which is an EU institution representing just 28 countries and based in Luxembourg.

When comparisons are made between geographical areas - countries for example – give some thought to the comparators selected: why for instance should one compare the NHS in the UK with the health services in Germany, Switzerland and Singapore as was done in a *Daily Telegraph* editorial[12]? [This editorial is referred to again in Chapter 7]. Why compare with two rather small countries and not say, France and indeed the USA? Given there are around 50 countries is Europe and almost 200 in the UN it's almost always possible to find helpful pseudo-comparators.

Financial Matters

Much of political comment and business coverage is naturally concerned with reporting on financial matters. A lot of sand can be kicked into people's faces with the devious use of data in this area.

Textbox 2.2 reproduces extracts from an article in *The Times*[13]. They are reproduced here to indicate the complexities of the public finances and as a warning that unless you are a geek you should be very wary of getting entangled in the nuts-and-bolts of national finance. These extracts indicate how it's important not to read too much into a change in the value of a variable if its value has been calculated by subtracting two or more large numbers. This is particularly true of the national finances. For example, the UK deficit is the subtraction of government spending of around £800billion a year from government revenues of roughly the same amount. Very small changes in either of these two large numbers can change a monthly deficit by a very large percentage. *The Times* article also provides an example of how the estimates made by experts can be wrong by £1billion a month, and monthly figures can be corrected by the same amount - not surprising when the Office for National Statistics bases its first GDP estimate on less than half the final data[14]. One-off changes can further cloud the picture.

Disinformation: identifying devious data and iffy information

> **Textbox 2.2 The Complexities of Public Finance**
>
> The gap between what the government spends and what it receives in taxes dropped by £700million compared with the same month last year, to reach £5.9billion.
>
> The figure was far below the £6.5billion economists had been anticipating. The deficit for August was also revised down by about £1billion to £4.7billion.
>
> John Hawksworth, senior economic adviser to consultancy PwC, said the improvement in the public finances was largely a by-product of inflation, which has raised the price of goods in the shops and increased VAT receipts, which rose 3.6% in September.
>
> Public finances are expected to deteriorate later in the year because a boost from self-assessment tax receipts in January and February will not be repeated as it was based on people getting ahead of a tax change on dividends.

Which financial measures to use? A difficulty arises about which financial statistics are most appropriate to cite as measures of national financial 'health'. This is too large a topic to explore in this book, but just to note that the measures do have fashions. Overwhelmingly, the measure that has been used over the last few decades to indicate the health of the UK economy has been GDP. This has been great for UK governments as the population of the UK has been increasing by the 100,000s each year for the last decade or so and this, coupled with inflation, has pushed up the headline GDP figures. Only of late has the per capita GDP been given any real emphasis. [It's reported[15] that the UK economy in 2016 was 9.3% bigger than it was in 2008 but only 2.1% larger on a per capita basis].

GDP is a very crude statistic. It only measures the level of marketed activity and so excludes all volunteer work (including child and invalid care). And GDP doesn't in any way measure quality: one country that needs to replace all the cars it produces after one year because of shoddy

Chapter 2 What's being reported?

workmanship will have 10 times the contribution to its GDP compared to a country that produces cars that last 10 years.

In the decades after WWII, the trade deficit was considered a very important measure and only recently has a renewed focus being placed on it. Productivity is another measure that has only recently come to be seen as vitally important.

The devil of inflation Inflation seems to be always with us and it can be used very successfully to mask true change. Two indices are in common use in the UK to measure inflation – the Retail Price Index (RPI) and the Consumer Price Index (CPI). Both indices are reporting the change in the price of a 'basket of goods and services' that are typical purchases of the British public. There are two reasons why these indices are different: what the baskets include and how changes in the prices of the baskets are calculated.

The RPI basket contains a large number of items that people buy that are excluded from the CPI. In particular, RPI includes housing costs such as mortgage interest and council tax, and other items such as vehicle excise duty and the TV license.

RPI and CPI are also calculated differently[16, 17]. RPI is simply the mean of the price rises in its basket of goods and services, whereas CPI calculates the average taking account of the possible substitution of cheaper goods for more expensive ones when relative prices change. Apples and pears could be considered substitutes. In calculating RPI any change in the price for apples would be directly reflected in the index: for CPI this isn't the case. If apples increase in price and the price of pears stays the same, the effect on the CPI will be more moderate than on RPI due to supposed substitution by households of one fruit for the other[18].

Why have two indices? Simple: the government loves it. The CPI is always lower or equal to the RPI due to the method of calculation: this is known as the *formula effect*. Over the past five years, the difference in annual inflation rates due to the formula effect has never been less than 0.5% and has been as high as 0.8%. This is why the government likes to link the payments it makes (pensions, train fare rises, business rates, student loans and so on) to the lower CPI and the payments it receives (eg. taxes) to the higher RPI. Interestingly, in September 2018 amid disquiet about imminent rail fare rises mandated by the Government, the Transport Minister[19] offered to raise fares by CPI rather than the traditional-used RPI to reduce the rise – but only on condition that the rail unions accepted the same index for their pay.

Exchange rates Like inflation, exchange rates are another great masking device. In the aftermath of the referendum vote in June 2016 shares in the FT100 index of the UK stock market (broadly the largest 100 qualifying companies) rose significantly. This was hailed in some quarters as a sign that the markets welcomed the prospect of Brexit. However, wiser heads pointed out that many of these large firms made their profits outside the UK and these profits were not denominated in sterling. Given the sharp deterioration in the sterling exchange rate following the Brexit vote, the profits naturally looked considerably better when converted into sterling. 14 months after the 2016 UK referendum, a commentator[20] in *The Times* writes about the UK economy that *…exports, aided by the drop in the pound, have risen by 16% since the referendum.* Given that the pound had deteriorated by around 15% against the euro and 10% against the dollar in this period, when looked at in euros or dollars this export performance doesn't look quite so impressive. Export <u>volumes</u> would be a much more valid indicator of export performance – but it wouldn't have chimed with the author's political persuasion.

From the foregoing it can be seen that it's very important to know which inflation measures are being used or if real figures are being stated (ie., figures from which the effects of inflation have been removed) and which currency/exchange rate has been applied.

Further issues

Average v marginal In Chapter 1 a lot of emphasis was placed on calculating averages, but we need to question whether in some circumstances an average is an appropriate measure at all. The cost and method of funding university education have been under fierce criticism for many years. Figures[21] cited for the premium earned by the average graduate from obtaining an undergraduate degree lie between £120,000 and £500,000 over their lifetime. Defenders of the system use these figures to send the strong message that it's in the financial interest of young people to go to university. The figures quoted are probably correct but the implication isn't. On the assumption that 'A' levels or equivalent are an approximate measure of academic ability, the financial test for any prospective student with border-line qualifications would be to look at the improvement in life-time earnings for the marginal student rather than the improvement for the average student. It's highly likely that the academically marginal student would be better off training to be a plumber, an electrician or other skilled tradesperson rather than studying a non-vocational subject at university.

Point value v. trend The media lives by reporting the latest news and unfortunately this quite often leads to an unjustifiable emphasis on ephemeral matters. In mid-2017 a *Guardian* article[22] about the new balance of the EU and the UK carries the statement. *How the tables have turned. Britain now appears to be stuck in the slow lane of a different kind of two-speed Europe. The UK economy has seen its slowest start to the year since 2012, as the Eurozone grows twice as fast. GDP growth was a tepid 0.3% in the 3 months to June, while the single currency bloc expanded at a much healthier 0.6%.* This whole article is based on a 3-month growth differential.

The transient nature of much financial reporting was also shown in textbox 2.2 and again in the story headlines from a Google search of 'UK house prices'.[23] It shows how crazy reporting can be, as there's a new story every few days or weeks, often at odds with the previous story.

Key points
- Be sure that you know what data is being reported on in a news item by asking a few basic questions. Surrogate measures have to be used in some instances: critically assess their appropriateness.
- Comparisons are made very frequently. Be sceptical if the comparison data – the time periods chosen, the comparator countries/areas etc. - don't seem obvious choices.
- Financial statistics are tricky, partly because there are so many of

Disinformation: identifying devious data and iffy information

> them. Concentrate on a few of the most significant ones, perhaps per capita GDP, the trade deficit and productivity.
> - Point values are almost always to be heavily discounted: look for trends.

Reports on House Prices

Date	Headline
07/08/2018	UK house prices hit record high in July despite 'soft' market - Halifax
06/07/2018	UK house prices grow at slowest rate for five years - BBC News
01/06/2018	House price fall here to stay, experts warn - The Times
31/05/2018	UK house prices dropped unexpectedly in May Nationwide
26/04/2018	UK house prices edge higher in April - Nationwide
29/03/2018	UK house prices fall for second month - Guardian
07/03/2018	House prices UK: Growth is 'modest' for February, says Halifax
01/03/2018	UK house prices fell in February, Nationwide says - BBC News
07/02/2018	Halifax turns downbeat on UK house prices Financial Times
06/01/2018	UK house prices fell in December says Halifax - first time since June
08/11/2017	House price falls now widespread, say surveyors
07/11/2017	UK house prices continue to rise strongly, says Halifax
06/10/2017	UK house price rises picking up, says Halifax
07/09/2017	Buoyancy returns to UK housing market, the Halifax says
15/08/2017	House price growth holding steady
07/08/2017	UK house price growth easing, says the Halifax
01/08/2017	Shortage of homes keeping prices high, says Nationwide
27/07/2017	UK house prices rebound, Nationwide says
18/07/2017	House price growth continues to slow in UK
07/07/2017	UK house prices fall further in June, says Halifax
13/06/2017	Typical house price up £12000 in a year, says ONS
01/06/2017	House prices fell again in May, Nationwide says
23/05/2017	Further signs of UK property slowdown in April
08/05/2017	UK house prices in first quarterly fall since 2012
28/04/2017	House prices fell again in April, Nationwide says

3 SAMPLING

> **The evils of bias and imprecision** Sampling is the process whereby a dataset is obtained for a portion of a population to represent the population as a whole. To get a good sample it's important to guard against bias and imprecision. Bias can be caused by such things as asking inappropriate question(s) or using self-selecting participants. Imprecision arises when the data gathering procedures are ill-specified or not adhered to.
>
> Common sense will protect you from falling for the most obvious failures in sampling but it can't be relied on in all situations. Possibly the best you can do is to look at the agency carrying out the poll. The standing of pollsters operating in the UK is referenced in Chapter 9.

It's very often the case that pollsters don't have all the data they would like to have. A classic case is the attempt to discover the voting intentions of the whole of the population of the UK. The pollsters would like to ask all 47million potential voters[1] how they intend to vote. However, it would be very expensive to do this – and indeed it may not be possible because of the difficulty in making contact with all eligible people. The best the pollsters can do is to look at a subset (sample) of the population and then work out what it means for the population as a whole.

In Chapters 1 and 2 we looked at descriptive statistics where the concern was with finding out important features of the group being measured. In the next chapter the concern is wider, expressed in the phrase *What does this situation mean more generally?* Thus we wish to build on descriptive data to infer something wider – we wish to extrapolate from a sample of the population to a description of the population itself. This extrapolation involves inferential statistics. Before plunging into inferential statistics – which we do in the next chapter - we need to explore the two major building blocks upon which such extrapolation is based. These are a) deciding which population is of interest and what we want to find out about it and b) deciding how to go about getting the relevant dataset on which to base our inferences. How to get this information requires us to consider samples and sampling. To make our discussion as concrete as possible we will be looking throughout this chapter at the conduct of the UK's 2016 EU referendum.

What's the population of interest and what do we wish to know about it?

In 2013 a Private Members' Bill was introduced into the UK Parliament to make provision for a referendum to be held on the UK's membership of the EU. The population of interest was all adult UK nationals. The question proposed was *Do you think that the United Kingdom should be a member of the European Union?* with the simple choice *Yes/No*.

This form of question was rejected when the newly re-elected Prime Minister David Cameron moved to start the referendum process in 2015. He was advised that the question caused confusion because many people didn't know whether we were in the EU and some people thought that the question was asking should we join! He put forward the alternative question *Should the United Kingdom remain a member of the European Union?* with the choice *Yes/No*. However, there were issues with this proposal as it only sets out the Remain option and the *Yes* response is for the status quo. It was considered that these features introduced unacceptable bias.

The Electoral Commission[2] then carried out a substantial consultation and testing exercise over many months in which 5 different question formats were investigated. The Commission's recommendation was accepted and appeared on the ballot paper: *Should the United Kingdom remain a member of the European Union or leave the European Union?* with the choice *Remain in the EU/Leave the EU*. So, quite an effort was made to get an appropriate question. This effort and the associated transparency were deemed necessary so that the result would not be contested as being unfair.

Chapter 3 Sampling

The importance of the wording in any survey is further exemplified by the excerpt of the account of a survey conducted by Opinium for the Social Market Foundation[3] reproduced in textbox 3.1. It's very easy to be inexact in a survey and consequently not know what the responses mean.

Textbox 3.1 The Importance of Wording

...Quite a few (of UK voters) are prepared take an economic hit to cut immigration too: 40% said lower growth and a bigger deficit are a price worth paying for lower net migration.

But 'growth' and 'deficit' are fairly abstract concepts, so we asked that 40% if they'd still want immigration cut to the tens of thousands if it means paying more tax or working longer before retirement. The people who still said those things were 'a price worth paying' are equal to less than a quarter of the electorate: only 21% back big immigration cuts if it means a higher state pension age...

Bias and imprecision in sampling

To get a handle on what's required when sampling it's useful to digress somewhat into considering 'inexactitude'. Inexactitude has two dimensions - bias and imprecision. Bias is a measure of systematic error, imprecision is a measure of random error. Both are very significant in getting an appropriate dataset from which to derive information about the population. To understand the influence of bias and imprecision within polling let's look first at a very simple example that may seem miles away from the sampling used by pollsters but which I think will be quite helpful as our discussion develops.

Four friends, Ann, Mike, Steve and Susie have a bet as to who is the best darts player. There's a certain amount of haggling over where to go to test this and how many darts to throw. They end up agreeing to go to the Blackthorn pub and for each to throw 6 darts aiming at the bull. [Note that each set of 6 darts is a sample of what's effectively a population of a very large number of throws].

Disinformation: identifying devious data and iffy information

The 4 friends exhibit widely different results, as shown in figure 3.1. Ann got the grouping shown in a). This tight grouping shows high precision – there's little randomness in where the darts land - but there's a large amount of bias. This bias could be because the set of darts has a systematic flaw, or because of some systematic way in which Ann throws. Contrast this with Susie's result in b), where both the randomness and the bias are very small.

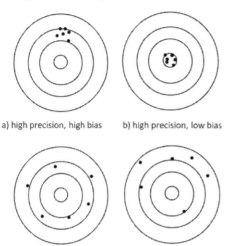

Figure 3.1 Imprecision and bias

a) high precision, high bias
b) high precision, low bias
c) low precision, low bias
d) low precision, high bias

Steve's result is shown in c). Eyeballing this diagram suggests that as the darts average around the centre the bias may well be low, but because the randomness of his throws is so high we wouldn't be confident in coming to this conclusion. [Contrast this with a) and b) where we can readily see the existence of any bias because the precision is high]. Mike's results at d) show how low precision masks how much bias might be present.

In darts we know where the players are aiming and that the disposition of the darts depends on the ability of the thrower, the environment and the soundness of the darts: in short we can say it depends on the throwing process. In sampling however, we initially have only a hazy view of the issue we are addressing and need to firm this up and have a clear question to pose. Then we need to select the process that will allow us to get the required dataset.

Suppose the 4 friends were pollsters with the same characteristics they showed when throwing darts. The situation is like that shown in figure 3.2. The circular 'blob' is the target issue, and the points are the results we might get from the respondents to our question(s). If Susie was a pollster she would have no problem getting the appropriate dataset as her bias is low,

Chapter 3 Sampling

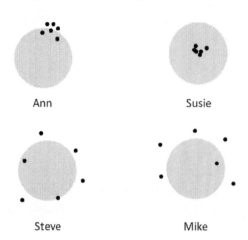

Figure 3.2 Polling exactness

and she could get this answer from a relatively few respondents (as her precision is high). Steve could increase the confidence in his dataset by using a large sample of respondents (as his bias looks to be low). However, Ann will find it impossible to get an accurate picture of the population – her dataset would be irretrievably too biased for this. The old adage applies - *Better to be roughly right than precisely wrong*. Ann is destined to get it precisely wrong - as probably is Mike.

With this understanding of the two elements of inaccuracy and some feel for the type of factors that influence them, let's now return to our principal concern – the UK referendum. We have a good referendum question and now we need to consider how pollsters might go about sampling.

The EU referendum – selecting the appropriate sample

With an unbiased question, the next requirement to get a valid dataset for the population is to select a sample that's representative of the whole voting population. There must be the correct proportion of each age group and gender, ethnic origin and place of residence and perhaps several more variables should be taken into account. This is a tall order. Fortunately in the referendum itself there was no sampling as the whole population was to be asked its opinion. However, extensive sampling was carried out in the run-up to Referendum Day.

A classic case of where a sample was inappropriately selected was in the 1948 US presidential election between the incumbent President Harry Truman and his Republican challenger Thomas Dewey. The major polls taken a few hours before voting had finished indicated Dewey had won – and the influential Chicago Daily Tribune carried the banner headline *Dewey Defeats Truman* on its front page. However, Truman won. Some reviewers believe that the polls had over-estimated the vote for Dewey because the pollsters had used telephone polling in an age when to own a telephone meant that you were relatively wealthy – and the wealthy were predominantly for Dewey.

Similar bias is likely to be present in virtually all polls conducted at websites and we must ask ourselves if these polls are telling us anything meaningful. The people who express an opinion are only the people who visit the website and who take the time to express their opinion. The participants have not been chosen to reflect any generalised population and the people who take part are self-selected and are likely to have common beliefs. The potential for bias is obvious. Textbox 3.2 provides a good

---

Textbox 3.2 A Website Poll

Almost 60% of grassroots Tories told the ConservativeHome website that the Prime Minister must fall on her sword after destroying her Commons majority. The results were described as 'astonishing' by the website's editor...

ConservativeHome received 4,763 replies in just 24 hours to its post-election survey on Mrs May's future – 'the second-biggest response and the most rapid'. Of those, 65% said the Prime Minister should go and 60% of Conservative party members said the same.

---

illustration of this[4] – the Conservative party was thought to have around 150,000 members at the time, non-party members could also express an opinion, and the 2017 UK election result was less than 48 hours old. So what was the value of this poll – except as a headline stealer?

Matthew Parris, an ex-conservative MP and a long-time member of the Conservative Party sheds more light on ConservativeHome when he writes[5] *ConHome is a haven for Brexit enthusiasts, dominated by the younger and more ideological kind of Tory, and pretty male. "Activist" is the right word for the ConHome community. "Activist" is, however, the wrong word for the national membership.*

Chapter 3 Sampling

"Grassroots" is better because Tory members are mostly anchored, unmoving, silent, subterranean and largely invisible.

Self-reporting Having selected an appropriate sample and produced suitable questions there always remains the bugbear of systematic errors often inherent when relying on self-reporting. It's been known for some time that when asked about the frequency of sexual intercourse people over-report the level of their activity – especially men. On the other hand people apparently very often under-report how much alcohol they drink. There's a very amusing Matt cartoon showing a woman saying to her husband when filling in an alcohol consumption form *I can't remember, does one reduce it by a third or a half on the form* - attempting to counter their doctor who will understand this underreporting and increase the stated level accordingly.

Imprecision in conducting the poll and the treatment of the collected data

The primary observer effect Let us assume that the pollsters have an unbiased question and have appropriately addressed any issues of systematic bias in the polling protocol – ie., the choice of respondents and the way the polling is to be conducted. The pollsters are still not home and dry however, as they need to ensure that there's little or no imprecision when their protocol is put into practice. One past error has been where pollsters go to an address, find no-one answering the door and so go to a neighbour and use their responses. You can see a potential imprecision here – selecting an excess of people who are out **of** work and fewer of those who are out **at** work. Or a pollster may not make much effort to contact difficult-to-reach people - poor people with no fixed abode or rich people who are holidaying out of the country. Perhaps the pollster conducting a focus group acts idiosyncratically, putting undue pressure on a respondent, putting words in their mouths or recording a response from someone who simply doesn't understand the question. This sort of protocol weakness is termed the primary observer effect - primary because it occurs during the data gathering process.

Disinformation: identifying devious data and iffy information

Secondary observer effect Rather than having an effect on the way that data is collected (as with the primary observer effect), the pollsters may impose their own idiosyncrasies on already-collected data and may shade their findings accordingly. This is the secondary observer effect. The implications of this behaviour could be significant. An interesting example of the way in which basic data has been modified in this way comes from the Office for National Statistics[6]. In order to prevent the frequency of domestic violence incidents by a relatively small number of multiple offenders distorting the underlying trends in the published data, the number of violent attacks by/on any one individual was capped at 5 per year. Thus any person who assaulted their partner every week would be recorded as making 5 assaults rather than 52.

High precision and sample size As we saw from the darts results, bias is difficult to identify if the imprecision of the individual outcomes is large: the 'noise' in the system prevents the true picture being clearly seen. The analogy of the steady thrower is a pollster who sticks to the protocol and so there's little primary observer effect.

From the darts example, we saw that a pollster with Steve's characteristics would end up needing to select a very large number of respondents to be fairly sure of getting an unbiased result: he would need a large sample size. Let's say that we want a sample in which 10% of respondents are to be adults under the age of 25. If we decide on an overall sample size of 30 people, then only 3 people in the sample will be under 25. Given that there will be a range of views within this demographic, a sample of 3 is very unlikely to mirror the views of young adults in general. The precision of the findings will be very low: a different group of 3 is likely to produce a different response. Indeed, if only one of the panel is an 'oddball' the poll results will be a very poor reflection of the under 25 segment of the population.

To take another simple example - tossing a coin and deciding if it's biased or not. In the long run an unbiased coin would produce 50% heads and 50% tails. If you tossed an unbiased coin 5 times it's perfectly possible to get all 5 as heads – and thus conclude that the coin is biased. If you tossed the coin 100 times, the chance of 100% of the tosses being heads in

Chapter 3 Sampling

an unbiased coin is well-nigh zero. It will in fact be very nearly, but unlikely to be exactly, 50%.

Sampling is an efficient means to get a dataset from which estimates about the population can be derived. To reduce the possibility of 'oddball' responses there's a need to take a reasonably-sized sample. In the next chapter we look at what a reasonably-sized sample looks like.

Key points
- Inaccuracy has two components – bias and imprecision. Bias is systematic error and imprecision is random error. Both will reduce the validity of a sample result.
- To reduce the amount of bias in a result there needs to be a clear framing of the question(s) asked and a clear identification of the target group.
- Adherence to a proper conduct of the polling will limit the amount of imprecision creeping into the sample. A small random error means that the findings of a survey can be identified with greater confidence.
- Any primary and secondary observer effects should be made explicit.
- Polls taken at websites are unlikely to have much credibility.

4 STATISTICS ABOUT POPULATIONS

> **Beware small samples and missing measures of confidence**
> Sampling is a way of getting accurate information about a population without spending large amounts of time and money assessing every individual. However, it should always be borne in mind that whenever a pollster or other researcher uses a sample to estimate the values for a whole population the results will be subject to what is known as sampling error: as the sample is smaller than the population it cannot be completely representative of it. When a population value is quoted it's vital that the sample size is stated together with the associated confidence level and margin of error.

Recall from the Introduction that the term population is the all-purpose term used for the totality of any collection of items – all the vehicles registered in the US say, or all the laptop computers ever made – and a sample is a selection of items from a population. Many statistics from a sample could be used to estimate the average of the population (mean, mode, median and others). Overwhelmingly the most common statistic that is used is the mean and conveniently the best estimate of the population mean is the sample mean. This is great and we might seem home and dry in finding the population mean.

However, suppose we wish to estimate the annual earnings for all full-time manual workers in the UK and have several people each taking a sample. One person taking a sample of 10 workers might get a sample mean of £19,250, another person taking a similar sample might get a mean of £19,750 and a third person might get £17,990. You can see that we are dealing with a probability distribution of these sample means.

Chapter 4 Statistics about populations

So the sample mean is only an estimate of the population mean and we need to know how confident we can be that it's a good estimate. To get a measure of confidence we need to know the way the data points in the sample spread themselves around the sample mean. Here again we have a choice but, because it can easily be manipulated mathematically, statisticians have elected to use the standard deviation. Thus to estimate the characteristics of the <u>population</u> from a sample the two <u>sample statistics</u> that are used are the sample mean and the sample standard deviation.

Because the terminology can become confusing I intend in this chapter to refer to the mean as the average and the standard deviation simply as the spread. Thus we will be considering sample averages and sample spreads and the population average and the population spread.

Note that because we can obtain a population spread doesn't mean that the true value of the population average can 'move about': it's simply that our knowledge of this true value isn't certain: possible true values lie around our best estimate of it – which is the sample average. Also bear in mind that we have actual values for the sample statistics but can only make estimates for the population statistics.

What we would like is a tool so that once we have taken a sample from any population we can use it to tell us how confident we can be that we have a close estimate of the population average. Figure 4.3 does this: let's see how we get to this happy position.

There are two aspects of sampling that are very significant in making life very much easier for the sampler. These involve first, the way in which individual items in the population are spread across all possible values – the shape of the population – and second, the 'law of large numbers'.

The importance of population 'shape'
Look at the two very different shaped graphs in figure 4.1. The first is the distribution of annual earnings. Consider what happens when you take a sample of, say, 10 items from this distribution: any extreme high or low values will be moderated by the more-numerous, more-central values. The majority of these 10 items will come from the areas where the probability of

occurrence is high. You wouldn't expect a second sample to give exactly the same value for the average, but again you would expect it to be near to

Figure 4.1a Distribution of annual earnings

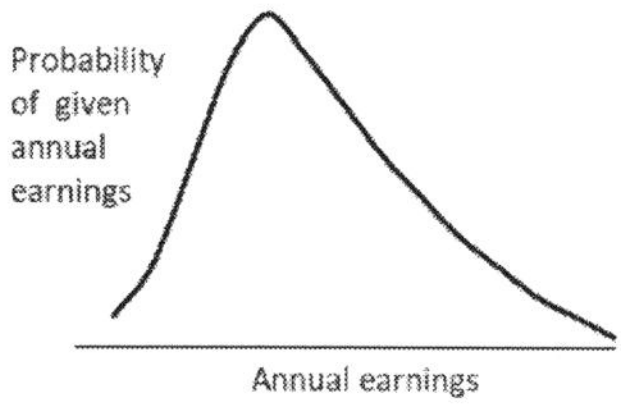

Figure 4.1b Distribution of days off sick

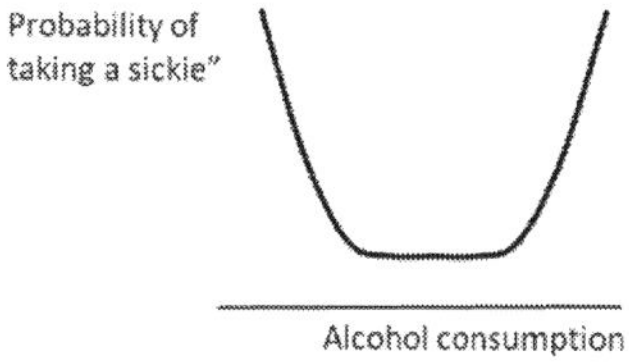

the first value because of the clustering close to the maximum probability.

Figure 4.1b is a diagram close to my heart, as it illustrates the finding that light drinkers[1] take less sickies than teetotallers! Even a distribution with this shape will provide sample averages that cluster about a central position. Furthermore, when you are looking at yes/no answers you get the sample averages clustering around a central position. If you toss an unbiased coin 10 times you could get the extreme of 10 heads and no tails (10/0) occurring but this would happen very rarely. Getting exactly 5 heads and 5 tails (5/5) would occur sometimes - far more frequently than 10/0 and somewhat more frequently than 4/6 or 6/4. The sample averages would cluster around 5, if a heads was given the value of 1 and tails a value of 0.

Figure 4.2 The 'bell-shaped' or Normal Curve

So intuitively we can see that there will be a clustering of sample averages. A very surprising thing that I hope you will take on trust is that for effectively all populations the distribution of the sample averages follows the same general curve – the 'bell shape' as shown in figure 4.2. This bell-shape is known as the *Normal Curve* and this most important result about sample averages is called the *Central Limit Theorem*[2]. The marvelous thing about this theorem is that it means that we don't need to be concerned about the form of the distribution of individual

Chapter 4 Statistics about populations

values in the population. The distribution in the population could be any shape – as the annual earnings, alcohol-sickies and coin tossing cases illustrate - and a normal curve would characterize the distribution of the sample averages.

The 'law of large numbers'

A second very important consideration in sampling is one that I hope is intuitively plausible. This is that the more values you have in a sample the better estimate you will have of the population average. As the number of values increases any extreme high or low values will be more and more moderated by the values of other, more-central and more-numerous items in the sample. Thus we become more and more confident as to where the true population average lies.

I will again have to ask you to take something on trust: that the link between a sample spread (which we know) and the population spread that we are estimating is:

$$\text{Population spread} = \frac{\text{sample spread}}{\sqrt{\text{sample size}}}$$

where $\sqrt{}$ indicates square root. Thus as the sample size increases the population spread decreases. A sample of 10 items will reduce the population spread to around one third of the sample spread: a sample of 100 items will reduce it to one-tenth. And of course, as the estimate of the population spread is narrowed we become more confident in the estimate of the population average.

The holy grail - the standardised normal distribution

We now know 3 things about all types of sampling:
- the 'shape' of the population we are sampling doesn't matter
- the sample averages cluster around the population average in a way characterised by the normal curve
- the population spread and the sample spread are linked through the square root of the sample size.

Knowing these 3 things we arrive at the holy grail of sampling –

figure 4.3. This is the standardized normal distribution – standardised because it's drawn in terms of a generalised population spread, and normal because it's the bell-shaped curve.

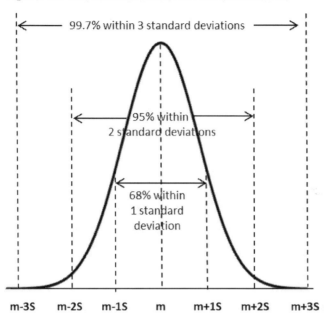

Figure 4.3 The standardised normal distribution

Figure 4.3 shows that the population average will lie somewhere around the sample average (m) - which is the best estimate of the population average - with, for example, a 95% chance of the population average being within ± two population spreads (2 S) of the sample average.

Confidence in an estimate of the population average – an example

In real situations only one sample would normally be taken. Let's say that our one sample of 10 workers produces an average of £19,250 for annual earnings with a sample spread of £4,520. This means that the best estimate of the population average will be £19,250 and the best estimate of the population spread will be £1,430 (£4,520/$\sqrt{10}$). In taking only one sample we are in a bit of a quandary. Is it one whose average is very close to the (unknown) population average or is it one that is quite different? Well of course we don't know. So what we have to do is see how confident

Chapter 4 Statistics about populations

we can be with the value we get. Naturally we use our sample values with the standardised normal distribution. The *confidence interval* is the plus-or-minus figure that is associated with an estimate of the population average. The *confidence level* tells you how much confidence you can have that the true population average lies within the *confidence interval*.

Using figure 4.4 we can say the following about the average annual earnings of the population:

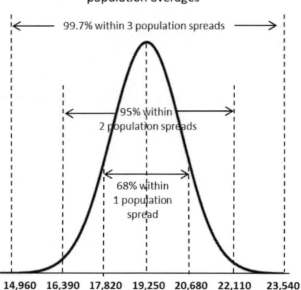

Figure 4.4 The spread of the estimates of the population averages

- With 68% confidence the population average lies within ± one population spread of the sample average (ie., the population average lies between £19,250 - £1,430 and £19,250 + £1,430).
- With 95% confidence the population average lies within ± two population spreads of the sample average (ie., the population average lies between £19,250 - £2,860 and £19,250 + £2.860).
- With 99.7% confidence the population average lies within ± three population spreads of the sample average (ie., the population average lies between £19,250 - £4,290 and £19,250 + £4,290).

Disinformation: identifying devious data and iffy information

Now whilst it seems clearer to use the term *confidence interval* in harmony with the term *confidence level*, the more common term – especially in reports of poll findings – is *margin of error*. Given its wider use I'll use *margin of error* from now on instead of confidence interval.

Put in terms of confidence levels and margins of error we can say:

- With a confidence level of 68% the margin of error is ± £1,430
- With a confidence level of 95% the margin of error is ± £2,860
- With a confidence level of 99.7% the margin of error is ± £4,290

The importance of sample size

Set out in table 4.1 is what happens to the margin of error at the 95% confidence level associated with our estimate of the average earnings of the population as the sample size is changed. Column 2 provides the 'formula values' of the population spread (with s as the sample spread) whilst

Table 4.1 Annual earnings : Effect of sample size on margin of error				
Sample size	Population spread	Population spread (£'000)	95% confidence limits (£'000)	Margin of error (£)
10	$s/\sqrt{10} = s/3.16$	4.52/3.16 = 1.43	19.25 ± 1.43	2,860
100	$s/\sqrt{100} = s/10.00$	4.52/10.0 = 0.45	19.25 ± 0.45	900
1000	$s/\sqrt{1000} = s/31.60$	4.52/31.6 = 0.14	19.25 ± 0.14	280
2000	$s/\sqrt{2000} = s/44.70$	4.52/44.7 = 0.10	19.45 ± 0.10	200

column 3 gives the numerical values. The margin of error narrows as the sample size increases[3]. Note the case of diminishing returns. As the sample size is increased from 10 to 100 the margin within which we have 95% confidence that the population's average earnings will lie narrows from £2,860 to £900 (a reduction of £1,960). As we increase the sample size to 1000 we narrow the margin further but only by £620. Moving to a sample size of 2000 only reduces the 95% margin of error by a further £80. This diminishing extra confidence when set against the extra sampling costs as the sample size is increased is the major reason why the typical poll to gauge voting intentions uses a sample size of around 1000. Only rarely is a sample taken which is much larger than this.

Chapter 4 Statistics about populations

Population size is unimportant

It may seem odd that the size of the population being sampled has not featured in our discussion. Only if a significant proportion of the population is contained within the sample is confidence in the population statistics likely to be boosted. [In the extreme of course, if all the population was included in the sample, there would be 100% confidence with zero margin of error]. Having a large proportion of the population in the sample is very rare and so to all intents and purposes the population size is irrelevant.

In mid-2017 Ofsted[4] reported adversely on the performance of Learndirect, a provider of training for vocational qualifications which had about 73,000 students on its courses. The CEO of Learndirect[5] tried to deflect criticism by saying that the 0.6% sample taken by Ofsted (around 450 students) was too small to justify Ofsted's conclusions: in other words the results could have arisen by chance and were not statistically significant. Superficially he might seem to have had a case, but statistically he didn't.

Significance and importance

A drug company has developed a new drug that it thinks has huge potential to bring about weight loss. It sets up a trial with two sample groups each of 25 people: one group is given the drug and the other – the control group – is given a placebo. Over the period of the trial the average weight loss for the 'drug group' is 8kg and for the control group it's 3kg. What does this 5kg difference mean if the drug is to be sold to the general population?

Note the value of having a control group. Without it the extraneous factors that are causing a 3kg weight loss in all trial participants (as shown by the control group) wouldn't be recognised and this figure wouldn't be subtracted from the effect of the drug on the drug group. Thus the weight loss due to the drug would be misreported as 8kg when in reality it is 5kg.

Recall the previous discussion: although the best estimate for the population average is the sample average, in any experiment that involves drawing a sample from a population the population average could lie anywhere within the normal curve drawn around this sample average. So the population average for the drug group could, for example, be a weight loss of 5 or 7kg and the population average for the control group could be 2 or 6kg.

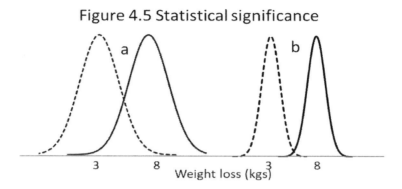

Figure 4.5 Statistical significance

Figure 4.5a shows the normal curves for each of these groups of 25 with the dotted line showing the distribution of the population averages for the placebo group and the full line that for the drug group. Note that the two curves overlap, meaning that whilst in general the drug does seem to be effective in causing weight loss there is a chance that it's no better than the placebo. The size of the overlapping portions is an indication of the uncertainty we have of the drug's effect. This uncertainty is expressed as the *statistical significance* of the finding that the drug produces a weight loss of 5kg more than in the control group. For a sample of 25 people the overlap is large and so we don't have much confidence in the drug's efficacy – perhaps only 60% - meaning that the 5kg difference could have arisen by chance on 40% of occasions had we repeated the trial many times.

Table 4.1 showed how increasing sample size reduces the margin of error. Increasing the sample sizes in the drug trial to 1000 say, would have produced the two curves in figure 4.5b. We would have considerably more confidence that the drug is really having an effect in this second case: the statistical significance might well be 90% or more as the overlap in the curves is so small. As is evident when you have a large sample size, very small differences will be detected as statistically significant. This means that you can be very sure that the difference is real: i.e., it hasn't happened by chance.

Chapter 4 Statistics about populations

Significance levels

Significance levels show you how likely a pattern in your data is due to chance. The most common level used to indicate that something is good enough to be accepted is 95%, meaning that the finding has a 95% chance of being true (and of course a 5% chance of being untrue). People sometimes think that the 95% significance level is sacred. This level comes from academic publications where a finding usually has to have at least a 95% chance of being true to be considered worthy of being labelled 'accepted as a fact-for-now'. In the business world if something has a 90% chance of being true it's almost certainly better to act as if it was true rather than dithering whether it might be false [as seems to have been the case in the Scottish Independence referendum – see later].

When statisticians say a result is significant it's short-hand for statistically significant, meaning it's a result unlikely to have occurred by chance: highly significant means the result is very unlikely to have occurred by chance. In normal English of course "significant" means important, but with statistics this isn't the case. Statisticians aren't saying anything about the importance of any results: importance is for the wider world to judge.

Under the headline *And we've become more cheery since Brexit vote* the *Daily Mail* reports[6] that happiness, measured in a survey by the ONS, reached 7.51 out of 10 in the latest study – up by 0.03 points on the previous year. This increase is almost certainly neither statistically significant nor important.

Making sense of poll results[7]

In the previous chapter we looked closely at the sampling procedure adopted prior to the UK referendum. We consider now what the results of the polls were telling us. In general such polls use a sample of around 1000 potential voters and quote their results at the 95% confidence level. The margin of error for such polls at this confidence level is typically 3% and we will use this value in what follows.

Polling prior to the UK referendum was a relatively simple affair since there were only two options – *Leave* or *Remain*. Throughout the run-up to Referendum Day the polls were close. In poll A the support for *Leave*

Disinformation: identifying devious data and iffy information

amongst decided voters was 53%: with a margin of error of 3% the pollsters would say that the support lay between 50% and 56%. This is depicted on the left of figure 4.6.

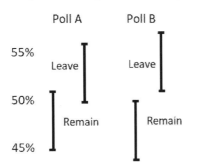

Figure 4.6 Significance of polls

For *Remain* the support might be stated as 48 ± 3%. As there is considerable overlap the pollsters would say that the difference in the returned results (53% v. 48%) was not statistically significant. In poll B however the 3% margins of error don't overlap and so the returned results 54% and 46% would be considered statistically significant.

In important elections polling starts well before the day of voting and many polls are taken in the run up to decision day. In this situation there is quite a good chance that one or two polls will give results that differ from the majority of polls: after all, the polls almost always use the traditional 95% threshold so we would expect 1 in 20 of these polls to produce results that differ from the population average by more than the margin of error.

As voting day approached in the Scottish Independence referendum in 2014 a YouGov poll gave the *Yes* vote a 51% - 49% lead, whereas all other pollsters were reporting *No* to be in the lead. This single poll, although not statistically significant, was enough to prompt the leaders of the main UK parties to revamp their offer to the Scottish electorate with 'the vow' – an enhanced offer to the Scots if they stayed in the Union. This revamped offer may have won the day – the vote split was 55% - 45%. On the other hand maybe it wasn't needed.

The sampling errors discussed here are those due to random factors[8]. As stressed in the previous chapter there is also the question of bias - the question asked in a poll, the way the sample is chosen and any data massaging - can all affect the published poll findings. So the differences between polls from different polling agencies may be larger than those

Chapter 4 Statistics about populations

arising from sampling error alone. For this reason, a run of poll results is generally more significant than the result from any one poll.

Key points
- The sample mean and the sample standard deviation are the sample statistics used to estimate the population values.
- Whilst the estimated population average is likely to be close to the sample average it is unlikely to be equal to it. This closeness is presented as the margin of error - the plus-or-minus figure reported with opinion poll results.
- The margin of error depends on the chosen confidence level which signifies how often the true population average lies within the stated margin of error. The most common confidence level is 95%.
- The margin of error increases the higher the required confidence level; it falls with an increase in sample size. Both features are reflected in the normal curve.
- The margin of error will fall the larger the sample size: correspondingly, the cost of sampling rises with larger samples. Sample sizes of around 1000 are typically obtained to strike the appropriate balance between cost and precision.
- Population size and population 'shape' don't have any substantial effect on how sampling should be carried out.
- Statistical significance isn't related to the importance of a finding.
- Control groups are vital in removing extraneous effects: without them research or poll findings may be fatally distorted.

5 ASSOCIATION, REGRESSION, CORRELATION AND CAUSATION

> **Beware associations and attributed causation.** Newspapers love to trumpet the latest 'research' findings – especially those linking health and social factors. Leaving aside the dubious way in which the underlying data may have been obtained, these associations aren't always statistically significant enough to use for prediction. And very often simple statements about datasets are expanded to imply that one factor causes another. A particular worry is the interpretation of the results from observational studies.

What we have been considering so far have been single variables – the heights of schoolchildren, annual earnings, voting intentions. This **is** a form of prediction as we move from the sample observations to make predictions about the population as a whole. However, there's another and wholly different area - where prediction involves estimating the value of one variable on the basis of its relationship with another. Textbox 5.1 gives examples of such relationships in newspaper headlines.

Textbox 5.1 Headline Associations

- Drinking red wine protects your heart
- Coffee drinking linked with intelligence
- High doses of painkillers 'raise heart attack risk in first month'
- Peanuts while breastfeeding 'help babies beat allergies'
- Stay married to halt dementia
- Women who have a regular glass of red wine found to be more fertile

Chapter 5 Association, regression, correlation and causation

Before moving on please note that whilst it's possible to make a distinction between the terms *association*, *link* and *relationship* I won't be doing so here – simply using these terms interchangeably.

Linear association One area where we might reasonably expect to see an association is between the weight of children and their height. Statisticians might say that there appears to be a linear relationship between weight and height - linear since a straight line can sensibly be fitted to the data. This line will encapsulate the major pattern in the dataset and allow for prediction.

A straight line linking weight and height will be of the general form

Weight = some multiplier of the Height + a constant

Put symbolically $W = a * H + c$

Statisticians use a technique called *regression analysis* to determine the values of the multiplier and the constant. It's too much to get involved in the intricacies of regression analysis here but it's worth knowing that the technique works by calculating the straight line that best fits the points by minimising the distances of the points around the line[1].

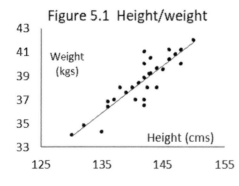

Figure 5.1 Height/weight

For the dataset of children's weights and heights the best straight line that can be drawn is shown in figure 5.1 and has the relationship (weight in kilograms and height in centimetres):

Weight = 0.4 x Height - 20

Great – we know the relationship! But we also need to know the confidence to place on it. Here we are talking about determining a

Disinformation: identifying devious data and iffy information

numerical value that sums up the quality of the fit between the values of two variables. Regression analysis is again the tool to do this.

This numerical value (usually labelled r and termed the correlation coefficient[2]) can be calculated to express the goodness of the fit. The value of r always lies between +1 and −1. The correlation coefficient will be +1 when the fit's perfect and when both variables increase exactly in step. For the weight/height relationship we would expect a positive correlation coefficient since increasing weight and increasing height generally go together. As the fit of the points to the line in figure 5.1 looks good we would expect r to be close to +1. The coefficient in our example is r = +0.6 – a reasonable fit.

Further examples of linear associations

Four scatterplots are shown in figure 5.2 to illustrate the types of linear relationships that might be encountered. An example of a perfect fit

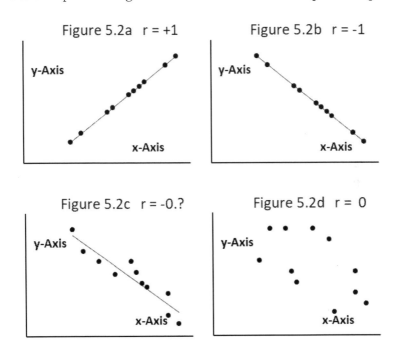

between two variables would be as shown in figure 5.2a, with r = +1. A second example of a perfect fit is shown in figure 5.2b but this time with r = −1, the negative sign indicating that one variable increases exactly in

Chapter 5 Association, regression, correlation and causation

step with a decrease in the other. It would be a mistake to think that a correlation of −1 is a bad thing indicating that no relationship exits: on the contrary, a correlation of −1 means the data is lined up in a perfect straight line. Figure 5.2c illustrates an association characterized by a negative correlation coefficient but one not close to -1 as the points are quite scattered around the best fitting straight line. The correlation coefficient will be close to zero when the relationship between the two variables looks like that shown in figure 5.2d.

We wouldn't expect most linear relationships to be so good that r would be very close to +1 or −1: real datasets aren't perfect. However, most statisticians would only say that there's a substantial linear link if r is beyond at least +0.5 or −0.5.

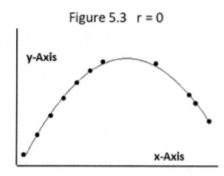

Figure 5.3 r = 0

Non-linear relationships Many things are linearly related and this allows us to sensibly calculate an appropriate correlation coefficient in a large number of situations. However, if a strong relationship exists but it's not a linear one, stating a correlation coefficient may be misleading. That's why it's critical to examine the scatterplots. The plot in figure 5.3 shows points that fit a line very well but it isn't a straight line. In such cases it may be possible to manipulate the variables to allow linear correlations to be calculated (for example using the square root of a variable instead of the variable itself). But then the meaning of the correlation becomes obscure.

Causation: fallacies in reasoning

Cum hoc ergo propter hoc When two variables are found to be correlated, it's tempting to assume that this shows that one variable causes the other. However, "correlation does not prove causation": if two events occur together this does not mean that one has caused the other. This fallacy is also known as cum hoc ergo propter hoc, Latin for "with this, therefore because of this." [Nice to get in a bit of Latin to show a rounded personality – like a well-known UK politician].

The association of storks bringing couples a baby is believed to have started in Germany several hundred years ago. Storks would fly south from Northern Europe in the autumn and return to nest in March and April. Babies born in March and April were likely to have been conceived in June of the previous year. Midsummer's Eve - June 21 - is a celebration of the summer solstice and it's also a pagan holiday of marriage and fertility. As many marriages and other couplings would take place then, many babies would be born around the time that the storks returned north, making the connection that "the stork brought the baby."

A second nice example comes from the letters page[3] of *The Times*. In this letter the CEO of the Creative Industries Federation points to research that shows that Nobel laureates in the sciences are much more likely to be painters, poets and musicians in their spare time than average scientists. He uses this information to push for creativity to be placed on a par with numeracy and literacy in education. He considers this research finding as 'proving' that arts involvement is an important feature of the laureates' scientific development – rather than the equally plausible interpretation that the laureates simply took up the arts in parallel with their scientific studies, took up the arts later in life or simply had more-wide ranging interests.

Figure 4.1b is a graph showing that less sickies were taken by moderate drinkers than by teetotalers. The rationale presented there was that abstaining from alcohol led to sickies being taken and that a small amount of alcohol was beneficial. Other, perhaps more plausible explanations are for reverse causality.

It's been found[4] that many non-drinkers in later life consist of ex-drinkers who have stopped drinking because of poor health. This is sometimes referred to as the 'sick-quitter' effect. Associations have also been found between persistent longstanding illness and persistent non-drinking suggesting that poor health from early age may be a reason why some people never ever take up drinking. This suggests that ex-drinkers and lifetime abstainers both suffer from pre-existing poor health and

Chapter 5 Association, regression, correlation and causation

therefore the relative better health outcomes from moderate alcohol consumption are not necessarily caused by the consumption itself or ill health by the lack of it..

And finally, an entertaining example from the pages of *The Times*[5]. An article appeared one day quoting a professor and clergyman who had made a study of hospital patients and noticed that more people admitted to hospital professed a religious faith than did the general population. He came to the conclusion *when people are confronting health, illness, and potentially end-of-life situations they may begin to ask questions about fundamental things that matter to them.* In a follow-up letter the next day another professor and clergyman pointed out that *what should be taken into account is the strong relationships between being sick in hospital and being old, and being old and being a Christian. The inference that people become Christian because they are sick is, to say the least, dubious. Notoriously, correlation is not causation.*

Post hoc ergo propter hoc A similar fallacy, that an event that follows another is necessarily a consequence of the first event, is the post hoc ergo propter hoc fallacy (Latin for "after this, therefore because of this"). The media are full of such stuff!

An article[6] in *The Guardian* illustrates this fallacy. It recounts the experiences of a school that introduced a great deal of music into its activities and then the school's performance in other subjects improved markedly. The view was that it was the music that caused this enhanced academic performance by making the students happier and more confident. This could indeed have been the case but other, more wide-ranging and controlled studies in education point out very strongly that it's the quality of the teachers that dominates everything else. Perhaps if some passionate science teachers had gone into the school the academic achievements would have been the same or better. Indeed a 2017 report[7] suggests that more school PE would boost children's brain power. (And see the description of the Hawthorne effect later).

The headline of textbox 5.2[8] gives a further example of the Post hoc ergo propter hoc fallacy. The follow up second paragraph however, unpicks the fallacy. The study involved observational research and such research can't determine cause and effect.

> **Textbox 5.2 High doses of painkillers 'raise heart attack risk in first month'. Drugs including ibuprofen increase peril by up to 50%**
>
> Commonly prescribed painkillers, including ibuprofen, increase the likelihood of having a heart attack within the first month of use if taken in high doses, a study suggests. For the paper, published in the BMJ on Tuesday, the researchers analysed results on 446,763 people over a decade on healthcare databases in countries including Canada, Finland and the UK, of whom 61,460 had a heart attack.
>
> But we must be careful of drawing the conclusion that taking painkillers caused heart attacks. For example, people who suffered the heart attacks may have been from lower socio-economic groups with poorer-than-average diet and exercise regimes. The use of painkillers and an increased incidence of heart attacks may have been coincident effects of a common cause (i.e. the disbenefits associated with a lower socioeconomic status) rather than a direct cause and effect, as might have been supposed.

Anecdotal 'proof' We have all heard things like the refutation of the deleterious effects of smoking on health with statements such as *Smoking can't hurt you. My Dad smoked 40 a day until he died aged 99.* And this sort of reasoning isn't confined to the bar-room. In an article[9] in *The Times* the author, after extolling the values of a history education for political leaders writes, *Nor are parliamentarians atypical among modern leaders. Lloyd Blankfein, chairman and CEO of Goldman Sachs, and Sir Howard Stringer, former chairman of Sony, both have history degrees.* This supposedly 'proving' something with a couple of examples is in fact only refuting the opposing proposition *No business leaders have studied history* – something I don't think anyone would try to argue.

Many news items – particularly those on TV and radio – feel the need to bring in the 'human angle' early on in the piece: dry facts need an uplift it

Chapter 5 Association, regression, correlation and causation

appears. But how often have you seen a TV reporter going to some way-out place like Ilkeston and asking apparently random bystanders what they think of some very complex issue – Brexit, should more money be spent on the health service, bombing Iraq? The opinion of a couple of people is then taken as a dominant view in that community. Anecdote trumps more considered evidence. Anecdotes can't prove anything – they can only disprove something. The saying *The plural of anecdote is data* is presumably said tongue in cheek.

Observational Research Observational research is a type of research particularly prevalent in the social sciences and in marketing, involving the direct observation of people in their natural setting. It differs from experimental research in which an artificial environment is created to control for spurious factors and where at least one of the variables is manipulated as part of the experiment. In physics for example, the relationship between the density of a liquid and temperature would be determined by controlling everything about the test liquid's environment and then measuring its density as the temperature is altered in a controlled manner.

Observational research is particularly good at unearthing emotions and behaviours – and it's the basis of focus groups. It may be better than using a questionnaire approach for eliciting emotions but the researchers' biases may intrude more as the focus group sessions are to some extent fluid and dynamic.

In observational research the researchers can operate covertly where they do not identify themselves, either mingling with the subjects undetected or observing from a distance. Alternatively, a more overt approach may be adopted where the researchers identify themselves as researchers and explain the purpose of their observations. The problem with this approach is that subjects may modify their behaviour when they know they are being watched – as seemed to have occurred in the famous Hawthorne experiment[10]. A series of experiments were carried out in the Hawthorne Works in Cicero, Illinois. Over a period of time the employees' working environment and working practices were changed in a step-wise fashion and the concurrent improvements in productivity were measured. The generally accepted interpretation of the outcomes is that the novelty of being research subjects and the increased attention led to temporary increases in the workers' productivity, not the changes in the working environment or practices themselves. This interpretation was dubbed "the Hawthorne effect".

Regression to the mean In the general election of 2015, the Scottish National Party won 56 out of a possible 59 Westminster seats. In the 2017 general election the SNP won only 35 – a loss of 21 seats. This was considered a resounding repudiation of the party's stance on a second independence referendum. The feelings on independence may well have been a very significant factor, but even if support for independence had remained the same it's unlikely that the SNP would have maintained its overwhelming dominance. This is because if an extreme result has occurred (such as the 56/59 MPs) it's very likely that this has occurred through a combination of the basic, underlying factors and a large dose of good luck. It's unlikely that such a large dose of good luck would occur a second time and the underlying features would then show up more clearly. This would certainly seem to have been the case with Leicester City and their exceptional winning of the English Premier League in the 2015-16 season.

An element of luck/randomness is common in many human activities. Lucky players with high ability will get extremely good outcomes: players with low ability and lots of bad luck will do very poorly. The luck is unlikely to be distributed the same way a second time and the players with extreme outcomes are unlikely to get extreme outcomes again, tending to get scores closer to the mean value of their group. This feature of statistics is termed *regression to the mean*[11].

Regression to the mean has significance for reward/punishment regimes. If someone scores very highly in a test it's common to praise them. Conversely, punishment may be meted out to those doing badly. Given regression to the mean, the next test is likely to see the high scoring person do worse and the low scoring person do better: praise will seem to have caused a reduction in achievement, whilst punishment will seem to have raised achievement.

Chapter 5 Association, regression, correlation and causation

Key points

- Correlation is the association between variables. A measure of the strength of a linear relationship is given by the correlation coefficient. A value near to ± 1 demonstrates a strong linear association; one near to zero a weak linear association.
- Two common fallacies in reasoning are to believe that because two things occur together or that one event follows another then there must be a cause-effect link between the two.
- Anecdotes don't prove anything: they can only disprove an assertion.
- Observational studies – involving direct observation of people in their natural setting – can't determine cause and effect: they can show the link between two variables but they can't show if one caused the other.

6 FORECASTING AND SCENARIOS

> **Beware detailed forecasts in turbulent times** The media are full of forecasts about almost everything under the sun, and when the future doesn't turn out as the forecasts predict, easy political points can be scored. This was particularly the case immediately after the UK's EU referendum when most of the dire forecasts for the UK economy failed to materialise – certainly not in the immediate aftermath of the vote. The forecasting tools used were called into question. One possible alternative is to abandon detailed forecasting in favour of scenarios.

In the last chapter we looked at how the value of one variable might be predicted by knowing the value of another. In such predictions time isn't a factor – in a sense such relationships are considered timeless.

A more daunting task is to attempt to predict the <u>future</u> values of variables. One way to do this is by simple extrapolation – by taking the relationships that have been found in the past and extending these into the future. This sort of 'blind extrapolation' makes the very dubious assumption - not simply that the future will be like the past - <u>but that the past is completely encapsulated in the data points that have been measured for that period</u>. This is likely to be very far from the case in a great many situations.

Consider figure 6.1[1] where 3 United Nations' estimates are given of the world's future population. The full line is a combination of the recorded figures for the world's population to 2010 and a simple extrapolation of this line - the UN high estimate. This high estimate simply assumes that the underlying causes that occurred in the past will continue into the future.

Chapter 6 Forecasting and scenarios

Rather worryingly this assumption leads to the prediction that the world's population will rise to 16billion by 2100.

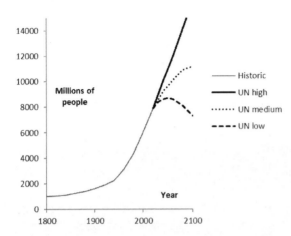

Figure 6.1 World population estimates

By contrast, the other two estimates are based on thinking things might be different in the future. To make such predictions requires that the situation is understood: that cause and effect relationships can be specified.

There are basically two ways of providing such a guide where simple extrapolation of past data would be inadequate: quantitative forecasting and forecasting based on judgement.

Quantitative forecasting A model is a representation of reality, either one that already exists or a view of what might exist in the future. It could be a model on a catwalk or the model of a concept car. But in quantitative forecasting we need to represent the situation in terms of mathematics so that we can readily make predictions – we need a mathematical model - which is a set of relationships written in symbols such as x and y.

A mathematical model is a simplified representation. A tiny example will illustrate what's meant by 'simplified'. Suppose someone sets us this puzzle: *Two identical twin boys are half as old as their widowed father and the combined age of the family is 80. How old is the father?* In solving this puzzle you will have thought something along the lines of:

Father's age + twice child's age = 80

A child's age is half of father's age

So father's age +twice [half of father's age] = 2 x father's age = 80

So father's age = 40

Disinformation: identifying devious data and iffy information

This may not look like it but it's mathematical – and would look more mathematical if we were to use symbols such as x and y for the ages. It's also a model – a simplified representation of reality. The full story is of identical twin boys and a widowed father. In producing the model you would have considered the twin information but you will have ignored gender, that the twins are identical and that the father is a widower. You would have ignored these features because they are irrelevant in seeking a solution.

Most forecasting models have many variables in them and some have a great many. The macroeconomic model used by the Office for Budget Responsibility[2] in the UK has around 550 - 570 with this number varying between forecasts. Some variables can appear quite esoteric. Consider textbox 6.1[3]. A few months after the UK referendum this article appeared in *The Daily Telegraph* quoting the views of Kristin Forbes, an American economist on the Bank of England's monetary policy committee. The author's overall concern in this article was to disparage all the economic forecasting around Brexit but he had a point in doubting two variables that the forecasters had used in their forecasting model, particularly the variable *media references to uncertainty*. This variable does appear rather esoteric and the source of the associated data also seems odd. It's valuable to query their inclusion. However, the selective removal of variables after the data has been collected and forecasts made can't be condoned: as is rather obvious, if you remove a variable that reduces an outcome you are bound to get an increased result.

The problem that economic forecasters had in the period around Brexit was that they were attempting to stretch the quantitative models they had honed over many years into a new and quite different situation. Thus they had to introduce new variables. Perhaps this was a mistake: perhaps they should have relied on judgemental forecasting – or the alternative which went under this guise – simply repeating bullish statements about the UK economy.

Judgemental Forecasting   Judgemental forecasting is appropriate when no suitable past data exists for meaningful quantifiable cause-effect

Chapter 6 Forecasting and scenarios

> **Textbox 6.1 Esoteric Forecasting Variables**
>
> How did the prediction gurus get it so wrong? According to Ms Forbes the Bank's forecasters systematically exaggerate the negative effects of uncertainty on the UK's economy, by measuring it using unreliable indicators. In particular, they give too much weight to 'media references to uncertainty' and the 'dispersion of growth forecasts', neither of which correlate well with actual levels of activity. By stripping these two indicators out, the Bank of England (BoE) prediction of future Gross Domestic Product (GDP) growth becomes 0.5% higher. That would turn the more pessimistic assumption of 1.4% GDP growth into the far more resilient 1.9% growth...
>
> You may be shocked to learn that two such crude factors, poorly related to what is happening in the real world, have such a striking effect on the economic outlook. It gets worse. Take the over-reliance on 'media references to uncertainty'. According to the BoE's 'conjunctural assessment' team, this is measured by the number of press articles citing 'economic uncertainty' that appear in just 4 newspaper titles – namely the *Financial Times, The Times, The Guardian* and *The Independent*. Hang on, I hear you mutter, but all four were editorially in favour of the UK remaining in the EU, and fervently reported all the harbingers of doom before the vote...

relationships to be developed (perhaps the situation after the Brexit vote). It's likely to be preferred as we look a long distance into the future. As can be seen from textbox 6.2[4] some judgements can be very wrong. Four of these forecasts were made by influential individuals in their fields. But using a group as in the fifth example is no guarantee that howlers won't be made. One way round this is to use 'separated groups'.

The rather pompous term 'jury of expert opinion' is sometimes used to describe people formally engaged in group thinking. The Rand Corporation developed the Delphi method[5] in the 1950s based on the principle that forecasts from structured groups of individuals are more accurate than those from unstructured groups. The method requires a panel of experts:

> **Textbox 6.2 Judgemental Forecasting Gaffes**
>
> 1880   Thomas Edison, inventor and entrepreneur: *The phonograph is not of any commercial value*
>
> 1920   Robert Millikan, Nobel prize-winning physicist: *There is no likelihood that man can tap into the power of the atom*
>
> 1927   Harry Warner, movie producer: - *Who the hell wants to hear an actor talk?*
>
> 1943   Thomas Watson, chairman of IBM: - *I think there is a world market for about five computers*
>
> 1985   Massachusetts Institute of Technology study Global Energy Futures: - *The supply of oil will fail to meet increasing demand before the year 2000, most probably between 1985 and 1995, even if energy prices rise 50% above current levels in real terms*

one whose members never meet and indeed don't even know who their fellow members are. Anonymity is maintained so that no-one slavishly takes their cue from an overly forceful participant. Each expert is asked their forecast on some issue together with their reasons for holding this view. A facilitator anonymises these responses and feeds them to all the other experts. The experts are encouraged to revise their earlier answers in the light of the replies from the other panel members. With appropriate rationale the revised estimates are fed back again in a new round of response-feedback-response and this cycle is continued until an expert consensus or something close to it is reached.

Melding judgemental forecasting with mathematical models The approach to building a forecasting model used by the Bank of England is outlined in textbox 6.3. Note that this approach marries the strength of both quantitative and judgemental forecasting.

It's very important to realise that the procedure outlined in textbox 6.3 puts the emphasis on understanding the logic of the situation first,

Chapter 6 Forecasting and scenarios

converting this understanding into a set of mathematical relationships and then linking appropriate data with the relationships to produce the

> **Textbox 6.3 Development Path for Models such as the Bank of England Forecasting Model**
>
> 1. A literature review is undertaken with input from sources such as the IMF and the OECD to help identify key economic trends, issues and risks.
> 2. Historical data is gathered on key economic variables.
> 3. This data is combined with the literature review to determine the relationships between variables.
> 4. These relationships are linked together to produce a full econometric model.
> 5. The model is used to generate forecasts.

forecasts. The logic precedes the data.

Big data and predictive analytics Another way of deriving an economic model is to look first at the data and identify relationships from the patterns within the data. Advances in information technology have allowed this search for relationships to be automated and, coupled with big data, has given rise to what's now termed predictive analytics.

There's an awful danger in using the big data/predictive analytics approach. If you put many datasets together then by chance a relationship between some variables will be thrown up. But are these real relationships? It's a bit like scattering a set of dots randomly on a piece of paper and asking people if they see a pattern in them. Often people do pick up patterns in the randomness: these patterns will be spurious given the way the dots have been produced.

As the Brexit negotiations developed during 2018 we witnessed a re-run of the pre-referendum situation. Using the Treasury financial model the Chancellor produced three forecasts spelling out in graphic detail the large financial downside to various forms of Brexit;. These forecasts were for the near-future and for around 25 years into the future. Dominic Raab who wrote the article in textbox 6.1 and was now the newly-promoted Brexit Secretary responded[6] by saying *I'm always chary of any forecast because most of them have been proved to be wrong.*

A forecast shouldn't be viewed as a target that's 'wrong' if it's missed: rather it's a 'directional guide' giving shape to the future. So Raab is probably mistaken to dismiss the Treasury forecast for the short-term as wrong since he must have known that the economy will almost certainly take a hit from Brexit. But Raab is probably right to reject such forecasting for the longer-term as adaptions will certainly occur as the future unfolds. For the longer-term we need another way of developing an insight into the future. Scenarios may provide this.

Scenarios The judgemental forecasting approach described above has been used successfully where single, specific issues are being addressed. Scenarios are a form of judgmental modelling that are generally much more wide-ranging. They are a (small) set of narratives each providing an internally consistent view of how the future may plausibly turn out. The narratives articulate the logical thought-processes underlying the proposed outcomes. Typically 3 or 4 scenarios might be developed when exploring the future.

Scenarios have been used by the military in their war gaming for very many years. Over the last two decades the use of scenarios has become a standard aid for strategic thinking and planning in many large organisations. Herman Kahn when working for the Rand Corporation says that the term 'scenario' was first used to de-glamorise the concept of writing narratives. The strategists emphasised that 'It's only a scenario', the kind of thing that's produced by Hollywood film writers – only a framework, not a blueprint.

Whilst a great many things could be considered in a scenario, the aim should be to concentrate on those that are important and where the strategic uncertainties are the greatest. A very simple example of scenarios is given in textbox 6.4 which is an extract from an article[7] that appeared in *The Independent* in 2017. Surprising as it may seem, this set of statements presents two scenarios *Before Brexit* and *After Brexit*.

Chapter 6 Forecasting and scenarios

Forecasts are predictions of the most likely way in which the future will turn out. In marked contrast, scenarios are simply vehicles for thought

> **Textbox 6.4 Boris Johnson and Leadership of the Conservative Party**
>
> Boris Johnson has worked out that his last big chance of becoming prime minister is if Theresa May falls in the next year or so... He knows that there are two ways May could go.
>
> The first would be if the Cabinet splits over the terms of Brexit. The reason he could be prime minister now is that he was the leader of the Leave campaign. That makes him the candidate best qualified to deliver Brexit if May won't.
>
> The second, after Brexit, would be if the party decides that it has the greatest chance at the next general election in 2022 under someone else. By then the party will be looking for someone who can win back the youth vote. In this scenario Johnson isn't a candidate.

exploration, both in their creation and use. The political problems of developing scenarios – or at least of making their existence know – can be significant.

At the Labour Party Conference in September 2017[8] the Shadow Chancellor John McDonnell revealed that one scenario the party had been investigating was where there would be a run on the pound immediately after the election of a Labour government. Not surprisingly, this exploration of a possibility was held up as a forecast – the most likely outcome. As Theresa May said in the House of Commons[9] ....*the shadow chancellor admitted a Labour government would bring a run on the pound and ordinary working people would pay the price.*

A second example of the confusion between a forecast and a scenario comes from *The Times*[10] with its headline *German army plans for EU collapse*. The article goes on to describe 6 scenarios that are being thought through of which the EU collapse is the most extreme. How misleading this is perhaps depends on what's meant by 'plan': normally a plan would be considered a fairly detailed set of future actions, which isn't what the German Army had been undertaking.

Key points
- Mathematical models are central to quantitative forecasting, particularly economic forecasting. They are simplified versions of reality with this reality represented by mathematical symbols and formulae and suitable for computer manipulation.
- Modifying quantitative models developed in stable times for use in future, more turbulent times is dangerous. Judgemental forecasting that relies on the views of experts may be more appropriate.
- A scenario is a narrative providing an internally consistent view of how the future may plausibly turn out. Narratives articulate the logical thought-processes underlying the proposed outcomes and it's these narratives and the breadth of their concerns that distinguish scenarios from judgemental forecasts.
- Forecasts provide guides to the future: scenarios provide a sketch of possible futures. In very turbulent times or when looking a long distance ahead, scenario building may be more appropriate than forecasting.

7 HOW DO THINGS COMPARE?

Beware a lack of context If you were told that the number of sausages consumed in Sweden in 2018 was 4million would you be amazed, concerned, anxious or feel some other emotion? Probably indifference, because a bare statistic without a way of comparing it with what might be considered 'the norm' is usually meaningless. You might become interested if you already knew or were told the population of Sweden, British sausage eating habits and so on. Very often isolated statistics are offered with a commentary that supports a line of advocacy that would be untenable if more information was provided. Context is everything when deciding if a piece of information might be significant or not.

Recently, an acquaintance told me he'd read that the number of murders and rapes in the UK over the past year had been 5million. In all seriousness he had calculated that he was bound to suffer some such fate in the next 10 years. What seemed to have happened here is that he had internalized a new piece of information without reflecting on what such a serious crime rate could possibly mean for daily life - he hadn't assessed the new information within a general wider context. [To put your mind somewhat at rest the total number of murders and rapes was around 1% of this number[1]].

In August 2017 the high master of St Paul's school and professor of later medieval history at the University of East Anglia wrote an opinion piece in *The Times*[2] under the headline *History teaches you how to run the country* extolling the virtues of reading for a history degree. The author writes that *over 10% of the (UK) cabinet are trained historians* and used this statistic to support the headline. Two errors of context were readily apparent in the article. First, when the article was published just 3 out of the 28 ministers who attend cabinet had taken a history degree. So the author's number just about holds up: 3/28 = 10.7% is indeed 'over 10%'. However, 5 members had Law degrees, 3 had studied Business, 3 Economics and 3 PPE. So it's difficult to make a special case for History. The second contextual error is that nowhere in the article does the author make a comparison with other legislatures – in Germany for example, leaders commonly have a legal or engineering background. This lack of comparison sits ill with the confidence with which the author extols the virtues of studying history, including the assertion that its study teaches how to marshal the available evidence!

These two examples indicate two aspects of the context needed to properly assimilate new information. The first is to bring to mind 'ballpark' figures - knowledge 'surrounding' the item's content - as should have been done with the crime news item. The second is to reflect on any comparisons that you could make when assessing a news item and consider whether any obvious comparisons have been omitted. Be especially wary when the contrasts are with an ideal rather than within the real-world.

Textbox 7.1 Sexual harassment 'at epidemic levels' in UK universities

Almost 300 claims against staff have been made in six years, but victims and lawyers say those are just the tip of the iceberg.

Sexual harassment, misconduct and gender violence by university staff are at epidemic levels in the UK, a Guardian investigation suggests.

Freedom of information requests sent to 120 universities found that students made at least 169 such allegations against academic and non-academic staff from 2011-12 to 2016-17. At least another 127 allegations about staff were made by colleagues.

Both these contextual deficiencies are illustrated in Textbox 7.1 where the opening paragraphs of an article in *The Guardian*[3] are reproduced. It

Chapter 7 How do things compare?

does look rather worrying, especially if you or someone you know is going to university. However, without context it's well-nigh impossible to make sense of the figures. So how are we to go about interpreting this news item?

Even one case of sexual harassment is too much but one of the first things to get a grip on is whether this is an unexpected figure. What might be 'the norm'? Questions might be:

a. What are the <u>rates</u> of harassment?

b. How do these figures compare with other, similar groups in the UK? Selecting comparable groups is fairly subjective, but without going into a breakdown of the composition of the student population at UK universities it would be a fair approximation to take it that the majority of students subjected to sexual harassment will be undergraduates aged between 18 and 22. How does this figure for UK undergraduates compare with those for 18 - 22 year olds in the general population? The same thing can be said about the staff – how does the level compare with what's occurring in the general community?

c. How do these figures compare with universities in other countries - with universities in other European countries and North America for example?

d. How do these figure compare over time? For example, with the 5 year period before 2011 - 12 - the most obvious period to look at. Calling the figures an 'epidemic' does suggest that there has been a sudden upsurge in numbers. [Such comparisons over time will be deferred however until the next chapter].

Whilst all these questions are legitimate it's not expected that you would have a lot of <u>detailed</u> knowledge about university life and harassment statistics, but when confronted by such a story the first thing should be to get a 'feel' for the data – the size of things. Using rough and ready approximations are all that are needed.

First, we see that over a 5-year period the number of allegations averaged around 60 per year. Whilst you are unlikely to know the number of universities in the UK you might consider the towns/cities in or near where you live, make a rough estimate of the number of universities there and do a quick and dirty extrapolation to estimate the total. A lower limit has been given in the news item – 120 universities. As we're doing a rough and ready assessment let's accept this number, so the sexual harassment level is very roughly one per university every other year. This doesn't seem much does it? You wouldn't be expected to know the average number of students at a UK university but, with around 100 universities, it's likely to be above 1,000 – perhaps even as much as 20,000. However, using what may well be - and actually is - a very low figure (only 1000 students per university on average) it means that only 1 student in 2,000 would expect to be sexually harassed each year. Even if the base rate in 2011 was zero, this is hardly an epidemic. Compare this with the TUC report[4] in which half of female workers said they had been sexually harassed. Taking account of a working life of 40 years say, this would seem to be a far higher rate than 1 student in 2,000. On this basis universities demonstrate a low level of sexual harassment, contradicting the claims made in the article.

The State of the NHS

A second example where context is vital in assessing a news item but where it's not given comes from an editorial[5] in *The Daily Telegraph* which is reproduced in full in Textbox 7.2. OK, you would expect editorials to be partisan but there are limits. Is this criticism of the NHS sensible and are the comparisons between the various health systems valid ones? Let's analyse the points that were made.

Leaking money, money spent and value for money No evidence whatsoever is given for the claim that the NHS is leaking money. On the contrary, studies[6, 7] by the US-based think tank The Commonwealth Fund found Britain's NHS to be the most efficient health service bar none amongst the 11 developed nations it considered. Of course there will be money wasted but this happens in all organisations. Using GDP at purchasing power parity (thus taking into account the relative cost of living rather than just the exchange rates) the annual spend per person on

Chapter 7 How do things compare?

healthcare in Germany is US$5,400 and US$7,300 in Switzerland, compared with US$4,200 in the UK[8].

Textbox 7.2 The State of the NHS

Given that the NHS operates as an old-fashioned state-run monolith, one would imagine that it at least has the structural capacity to implement improvements from the centre. Far from it. In an interview with this newspaper, Prof Sir Bruce Keogh, the service's medical director, says that patients are being endangered by the lack of a central system for ordering changes to practice based upon safety concerns. The NHS might leak money like a monolith, but it operates like a "conglomerate of hundreds of organisations".

A near record number of so-called "never events" were reported in the NHS last year, things that needn't happen and shouldn't happen, but do. There were 18 cases of an operation being carried out on the wrong knee. Surgical swabs were mislaid inside patients 22 times and three patients fell out of windows. And last month, the Care Quality Commission issued a report indicating that around a third of GP surgeries have put patients at risk. A man in a Brighton practice was found to be doing the work of a GP despite having no medical qualifications.

The Government has done its best to improve the NHS by, for example, imposing league tables of performance. It doesn't help that the institution is at once enormous and unscalable, yet devolved and difficult to govern. Worse, it is protected by the myth that it is "our NHS" – a moral crusade – and thus this basic flawed structure is beyond criticism. The sorry truth is that whatever is done to the NHS, more centralisation or less, nothing will ever really work. Other systems – Germany's, Switzerland's, Singapore's – are better. Real change will only begin by admitting this fact.

Disinformation: identifying devious data and iffy information

These are extra expenditures of 30% and 75% respectively. The writer could have chosen the USA as a comparator: here annual per capita health spending is US$9,600 - 130% more than in the NHS. In short, the NHS provides very good value-for-money. And it should be borne in mind that this performance is in the UK where national productivity is low by international standards[9].

Never events and other failures The use of the term 'never event' is unfortunate since it suggests that the occurrence of such an event would always be life-threatening, but this isn't the case in the majority of the event categories. In any organisation where human interaction is significant, as in the NHS, we should expect some errors to occur. The writer fails to give figures for any other health systems, making the implicit comparison with perfection. (The author's assertion puts me in mind when estimates were made of the Soviet threat to NATO in the 1970s: it was lamented that British tanks would break down and that NATO aircraft would often be out of service needing maintenance. If you weren't careful, you assumed that no Warsaw Pact tank ever broke down, no Soviet unit ever lost its way, communications were perfect and Russian soldiers were 10ft tall).

What wasn't mentioned in the editorial was that in the 10 months between 1st April 2016 and 30th January 2017 there were only 351 never events in all of England's hospitals[10]. This is about 1 per day. In the year 2013/4 4.7million surgery admissions were made in England[11]. The hospital with the largest number of never events was Barts Health NHS Trust in London with 10 incidents. This hospital carried out 80,000 surgical procedures in that period.

User satisfaction and medical outcomes Other health systems – Germany's, Switzerland's and Singapore's - are considered to be better. The Commonwealth Fund findings do concentrate on survey data of patient and clinician experience rather than health care outcomes. On medical outcomes the NHS is just above the US at the bottom of the table. It's difficult to identify the cause of this poor showing because countries have different health cultures: for example, UK residents are the third fattest in Europe[12].

Chapter 7 How do things compare?

One major medical outcomes measure was *mortality amenable to medical care* (deaths which could have been avoided) with the best performing nation (Switzerland) about 50% better than the UK. The irony is that if the author had properly accessed the available databases they could perhaps have made a reasonable case for their claim based on this medical outcomes measure (but see later in this chapter).

The evidence in textboxes 7.1 and 7.2 illustrate the need to view information in the context of 'the norm'. And the norm requires the sources of any data to be acknowledged. The sexual harassment article does cite the source but doesn't then make any valid comparisons. The editorial seems simply to have cited one or two examples of failure and then moved on to preach unrestrainedly to the converted. At the end of this piece there's the bold assertion *nothing will ever really work*. The evidence as given in the editorial in no way sustains this view.

Absolute and relative measures There are two main ways of comparing sets of data. If this comparison is made on the raw data then it's an absolute measure: if it's made in terms of proportional or percentage differences then it's a relative measure.

A report that uses relative measures is likely to make for arresting headlines and this seems particularly prone to happen when health scares and medical advances are reported. An example of the absolute and relative measures follows on from the NHS article (textbox 7.2). On the relative measure of *mortality amenable to medical care* Switzerland is about 50% better than the UK. However, the absolute rates are around 0.5 and 0.8 deaths per 1,000 people (ie., 0.3 extra deaths per 1000 people), giving a rather different slant on the findings I think you'll agree.

The excerpt in textbox 7.3 again dips into the *The Guardian*[13] article first referenced in Chapter 5. Given that ibuprofen is very widely used and generally considered a fairly safe painkiller, this news could appear very frightening to many people. But what's the article telling us?

> **Textbox 7.3 High doses of painkillers 'raise heart attack risk in first month'. Drugs including ibuprofen increase peril by up to 50%**
>
> Commonly prescribed painkillers, including ibuprofen, increase the likelihood of having a heart attack within the first month of use if taken in high doses, a study suggests.
>
> The overall odds of having a heart attack were about 20% to 50% greater if using non-steroidal anti-inflammatory drugs (NSAIDs) compared with not using the drugs.

What it's not telling us is that the chance of having a heart attack is at least 20%. In fact it isn't telling us anything sensible about the chances of having a heart attack. And the reason it isn't is that we aren't given any information about the chances of a heart attack without the painkillers or before the use of the painkillers started: we aren't given what's termed the base rate figures. It's obviously very important to know that the overall risk is low, amounting to about a 1% chance of having a heart attack in a year if taking the tablets daily. Whilst individuals may consider a 1% chance as being important, it's a far cry from 'up to 50%'. [In fairness to the Guardian article it put in the following quote from a pharmacologist towards the end of the article *The two main issues here are that the risks are relatively small, and for most people who are not at high risk of a heart attack these findings have minimal implications.* This form of reporting seems to be becoming more prevalent: the headline and body of the news item are based on relative measures whilst the absolute consequences are mentioned only in the last couple of lines.

This use of relative measures rather than absolute ones has even infected *The Lancet*, the UK's foremost journal for recording the results of medical research. In 2018 it published a review[14] of many reports on the effects of alcohol consumption on 23 major diseases. The results were reported in many media outlets along the lines of *There's no safe limit for alcohol use*. This was an apt heading to the extent that there was no 'dip' in

Chapter 7 How do things compare?

risk with increased alcohol consumption (unlike figure 4.1b). This view was based on relative measures – the risk of getting a disease versus the risk for teatotallers. But the conclusion of no safe limit was excessive. Analysing further the basic data to expose the absolute level of risk showed that for every 25,000 people having one drink a day (roughly one UK unit of alcohol) one extra person would get one of the major diseases in that year. So, perhaps there is no safe limit – where safe means no risk - but then there isn't a safe limit for bus travel either.

Percentage changes vs percentage point changes In 2018 the amount that was spent by the UK's National Health Service was approximately £150billion whilst the GDP was approximately £2,000billion. Suppose the Chancellor is to decrease health spending by £15billion in the next financial year. They could announce this is at least 3 ways:

a) simply as a reduction of £15billion.

b) as a percentage change in the previous amount spent on health – a 10% reduction.

c) as a percentage point change – the change in the proportion of GDP spent on health - would decrease from 7.50% to 6.75%, a change of 0.75%.

Note that in a) they would be announcing an absolute decrease; in b) they would be announcing a relative change in health spending; in c) they would be announcing a change in health spending as a % of GDP. No prizes for guessing which announcement they would prefer to make. They could pass off a change that's likely to have serious consequences for the NHS as simply reducing the health spend by *less than 1 percentage point*. Politically irresistible.

Making sense of national statistics What became evident in the build up to the Brexit vote was how ignorant people were of the size and makeup of the national finances. One of the most telling examples of this ignorance was the slogan on the side of the Brexit bus *We send £350million to the EU every week*. Although this figure has been shown to be wrong, the purported correct figure (£280million) was also considered enormous. The debate about which figure was correct only convinced more and more people that the money 'wasted' on the EU was indeed vast. But is it? The GDP for the UK in 2016 was around £2,000billion. Even at £350million per week (£18billion per year) the amount sent to the EU is under 1% of GDP. Obviously no-one wants to waste/lose any part of GDP but these figures were not huge economically. But as it proved, they were huge politically.

What this leads onto is that in order to make sense of a great many news items it's vital that you know the broad contours of the national economy, so that they can be referred to quite naturally as you assess an item. There's no requirement for precision – (very) rounded figures are all that's required.

Key points

- You read/see a news item to acquire information. The value of this information is only realised when you mesh it with other information to produce knowledge - a rounded view.
- Beware 'lonely data'. Always try to place an individual piece of data in context.
- Much context involves contrasts. Contrasts with ideal states or situations are seldom of value – human activities and institutions are always imperfect.
- One very important broad recommendation is to discount relative measures where the associated absolute measures aren't stated.
- Always look for 'per'. GDP per person is much better measure than GDP: the number of incidents of knife crime in London is a much less useful statistic than knife crime incidents per head of population.

Chapter 7 How do things compare?

A little Quiz

Here is a little quiz on the UK economy in the financial year 2017-2018, and then figures for the world as a whole[15]. (Answers are given in the end notes[16]).

A. What is the size of the UK economy (its GDP)?
B. What is the population of the UK?
C. What is the total UK military defence spend per year?
D. What percentage of the UK economy is the agriculture sector?
E. What proportion of the UK population is Muslim?
F. What is the total NHS spend per year?
G. What is the total UK governmental education spend per year?
H. What percentage of the UK economy is the manufacturing sector?
I. What is the population of Scotland?
J. What is the population of the EU without the UK?
K. How does the land area of the UK compare with that of France?
L. In the last 20 years the proportion of the world population living in extreme poverty has a) almost doubled, b) remained more or less the same, c) almost halved.
M. What is the life expectancy of the world today? a) 50 years, b) 60 years, c) 70 years, d) 75 years?
N. How many people in the world have some access (possibly intermittent) to electricity?
O. What is the world population expected to be in 2040?
P. Of the 7billion people in the world today, how many live in the Americas? In Africa?

8 HOW ARE THINGS PROGRESSING?

Carefully scrutinise the time periods chosen for comparison In the previous chapter we explored the importance of context in adding meaning to data and saw context as a comparison with similar areas – geographical, social, political and economic. We were addressing the question – *How do things compare to those in other areas?* In this chapter we will explore the context of time - how data over a period of time can be used to answer the question *How are things progressing?* We'll look first at how the pairing of data is so influential in presenting a case and then move on to see how using all the data in a time series can be more illuminating. Then, using the example of global warming, we will look at how partial graphical data can be use so mischievously.

In his State of the Union Address[1] one year after he became POTUS, President Trump declared *Since the election, we have created 2.4 million new jobs, including 200,000 new jobs in manufacturing alone. Tremendous number.* Was this boast valid or the dreaded 'fake news' he so often accuses his detractors of spreading? Could he be especially proud of these figures?

Factcheck[2] has looked at this claim and found that since October 2016, just before Trump was elected at the beginning of November, 2.37million jobs were created. But Trump didn't take office until the 20th January 2017. The gain since Trump took office was 1.84million: for manufacturing jobs the corresponding increase was 184,000.

So what can we say about Trump's claim? Well, although the numbers of jobs created are somewhat inflated they are reasonable, and rounding is the appropriate thing for such a public statement. But the implications of

Chapter 8 How are things progressing?

what he said aren't reasonable. The problem is that he has simply quoted two isolated figures: what he wanted his audience to think was that these were extraordinarily good figures. Whilst comparisons could have been made with the number of jobs created in similar countries, the most obvious comparison is with the jobs created by his predecessor, President Obama. In fact, the pace of jobs growth actually slowed 12% during Trump's first 11 months in office compared with the preceding 11 months[3].

Although lacking valid comparisons as least Trump's assertion specify the time period he was talking about – his first year in office.. This is certainly superior to the way in which Nick Gibb the (Conservative) UK Schools Standards Minister had announced the improvement in literacy scores for children in England. He was rebuked by the Sir David Norgrove[4], chair of the UK Statistics Authority who complained officially:

Nick Gibb claimed last week that the UK had "leapfrogged up the child literacy rankings last year, after decades of falling standards, going from 19th out of 50 countries to eighth". In fact, the improvement was significantly smaller – from 10th place in 2011 to eighth in 2016. The greater rise, from 19th to 10th, took place between 2006 and 2011 – mostly under Labour governments.

Note the missing time fame in Gibb's misleading statement.

All politicians want to show that things have improved on their watch – for example, that crime rates are falling, productivity is rising. When they wish to show that something has changed it's obvious that they should state the time period over which they are claiming the change has occurred, otherwise their claims will be meaningless or misleading. Usually, the best way to give credibility to the start and end points of any time period is to tie them to significant events – and for politicians this would generally be political or economic events. Due to political and media pressure, end dates would normally have to be either the latest official figures or current estimates. However, there's a fair amount of leeway for the start dates. As we move towards the next general election in the UK obvious start dates are the dates of previous UK elections – May 2010, May 2015 and June 2017. Perhaps the EU referendum date of June 2016 might be used or, in Scotland, its referendum of September 2014. Perhaps going back into the Labour Government's figures prior to 2010. [Note that Trump did

Disinformation: identifying devious data and iffy information

have start and end dates but these were simply to bracket the numbers – he didn't explicitly compare performance over time].

Let's explore ways in which politicians can show things have improved by considering the quarterly UK GDP figures[5] as set out in in table 8.1.

Table 8.1 % change in GDP for the UK					
	Q1	Q2	Q3	Q4	Annual
2010	0.7	1.9	2.2	2.0	1.7
2011	2.0	1.3	1.2	1.3	1.5
2012	1.4	1.1	1.9	1.5	1.5
2013	1.5	2.2	1.9	2.6	2.1
2014	2.8	3.1	3.0	3.3	3.1
2015	2.7	2.5	2.1	2.1	2.4
2016	1.9	1.8	2.0	2.0	1.9
2017	2.1	1.9	1.8	1.4	1.8

Let's take the end date as the most recent one in the series – the last quarter (Q4) of 2017. In a comparison of GDP growth we could contrast the 1.4% in that quarter with:

- the quarter in 2010 containing the May election (Q2) – 1.9%
- the quarter in 2015 containing the May election (Q2) – 2.5%
- the quarter in 2017 containing the June election (Q2) – 1.9%

The weakness of all 3 comparisons for a government spokesperson is obvious – they certainly shouldn't compare the GDP growth in Q4 of 2017 with any of these earlier quarters. But wait – there are possibilities: in Q1 just prior to the May 2010 election a growth of 0.7% was recorded, so it could legitimately be claimed that the growth in Q4 of 2017 is twice the growth just before the Conservative-dominated coalition took office. Another feature that a government spokesperson could have stressed is the increase in the annual growth rates between 2010 and 2017 – a small increase, but an increase nevertheless.

Textbox 8.1 is an extract from a column in *The Times*[6] illustrating the many ways a story can be told, depending on the time period selected for comparison.

Chapter 8 How are things progressing?

> ### Textbox 8.1 The fluctuating economy
>
> Growth is down. The UK economy expanded month-on-month by only 0.1 per cent in June. No, growth is up. The economy grew by 0.4 per cent in the quarter to June, up from 0.2 per cent in the previous quarter.
>
> No, growth is flat. The economy grew at exactly the same pace in the first half of this year as in the second half of last year. No, growth is down. We are on "a trend of slowing growth since 2014", the Office for National Statistics says.

From these examples we can see that there are many ways pieces of data can be paired to show almost whatever outcome you wish to show. The devious can really get going. Recall from chapter 2 the craftiness of Mrs May in choosing an advantageous time period for her comparison of police pay. The main issue with individual bits of data is that so little of the available data is used, and so the information contained in all the data taken together isn't revealed. What if we used all the data points available rather than just two – or in Trump's case just one?

Data series: signal and noise

The GDP dataset set out in table 8.1 is a time series – a set of data points at equally spaced time periods. This dataset contains within itself longish-term trends. The trouble is that any trend is being (partly) masked by the randomness in the data. This randomness is like noise at a party, the noise hides and distorts the conversation you're trying to listen to. We explored this randomness in chapter 4 in connection with samples: here we explore it in connection with a time series.

Figure 8.1 shows the UK quarterly GDP time series spanning the global recession of 2007-10. Is there a trend here? How can we unearth any messages there may be in the data? We could do as was done in chapter 5 and use regression analysis to fit a straight line to the data. But why should we imagine that the growth in GDP would be linear[7]? So let's not make any assumptions about linearity and see if we can extract the trend from the noise. The most common way to do this is by smoothing the data. This can be done in a number of ways but by far the most common is to use a moving average [it's actually the moving mean but no-one ever seems to call it that].

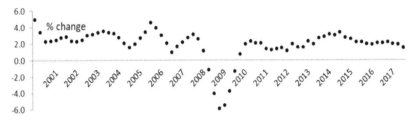

Figure 8.1 Quarterly % change in UK GDP

Moving averages

The annual average for the 4 quarters of 2010 is 1.7%. This value would be most applicable to the mid-point of the 4 quarters – the mid-point of 2010. Suppose the % change in GDP for the first quarter (Q1) of 2011 becomes available. The average could now be recalculated using Q1 of 2011 rather than Q1 of 2010, and the new average would be the average of quarters 2, 3 and 4 of 2010 and Q1 of 2011 (1.9, 2.2, 2.0 and 2.0 averaging 2.0%). The next moving average would be composed of Q3 and Q4 of 2010 and Q1 and Q2 of 2011 – averaging 1.9%. This average is 'moving' because it's continually recalculated as new data becomes available: the earliest value is dropped and the latest value is included to form the new average. This moving average for the whole of the period 2010 to 2017 is shown in figure 8.2.

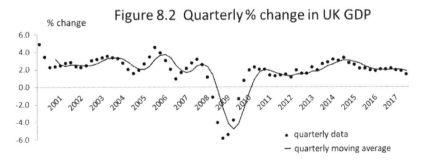

Figure 8.2 Quarterly % change in UK GDP

Chapter 8 How are things progressing?

The moving average in figure 8.2 has been calculated by using the 4 quarters of a year to form each average: we have used a 'window' of a year and moved this window along the data series calculating a new average as a more recent data point is included. This means that any seasonal effects will be suppressed because each season is represented in each average.

Moving averages reduce both the effect of temporary and random variations in data and improve the 'fit' of data to a line to show any trend more clearly. As we have seen, one characteristic of moving averages is that if the data has a periodic fluctuation, then applying a moving average of that periodicity will eliminate that variation (the average always containing one complete cycle). Of course, this elimination is usually exactly what's sought.

A major drawback of using a moving average is that it lets through a significant amount of the fluctuations shorter than the window length. This can lead to unexpected mismatches such as the smoothed result lagging behind the raw data. Figure 8.2 illustrates this point. Notice the lagging as the recession took hold in 2007 and that the smoothed rise from late-2013 to early-2015 lags behind the data points by about 2 quarters. Note also that the latest smoothed values haven't picked up the apparent downturn in the quarterly figures in 2017.

Before moving on to other representations of time series note that in chapter 6 two main ways of forecasting were considered – simple extrapolation of the past data without considering any underlying factors, and forecasting where known cause and effect relationships are used to estimate future values. Whilst this chapter isn't concerned with forecasting but of making sense of known data series, there are the same two ways of looking at the data – simply fitting a curve to a time series, as is done with smoothing, or trying to make sense of the time series through an understanding of the underlying cause and effect associations.

Graphical (mis) representation of data series.

We saw earlier in this chapter how the clever/devious selection of pairs of data could considerably affect how a situation might be presented. We also saw how smoothing could be a part of the answer to deviousness by

Disinformation: identifying devious data and iffy information

showing up any longer-term trend by using more of the data. Now we will look at how selecting partial graphical information from a time series can also be used selectively, and how this selectivity can be exposed and removed.

President Trump was filmed coming out of his hotel in New York on a very cold mid-winter's day in 2017 and remarking *And they talk of global warming!* Here he showed the confusion – either real or concocted – between weather and climate. Weather is the day-to-day meteorological conditions (such as temperature, rainfall and wind speed) affecting a specific place. Climate is the general weather averaged over a long period of time and over a substantial geographical area. We will be using the most important aspect of climate change[8] - global warming – as an example of how the information in a data series can be presented.

Climate scientists, politicians and indeed climate change deniers want us to know the trend in global temperatures. Any temperature change has a climate component and a weather component. We can consider the climate component as a signal with the weather creating the noise. The signal to noise ratio is a very useful concept: it's a measure of the strength of the signal compared to the amount of noise.

Signal and noise

Two time series of 5 annual temperatures are shown in figure 8.3.

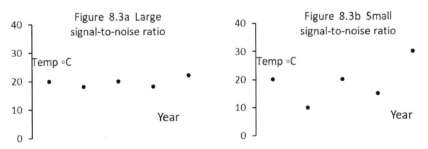

These are annual values so seasonality is absent. In figure 8.3a the signal-to-noise ratio is high and only the statistically pernickety would be likely to challenge you if you said that the trend is flat. In figure 8.3b the signal-to-noise ratio is so small (because the noise is so large) that any signal is lost in the noise: it's quite possible for the temperature trend to be rising, falling or

Chapter 8 How are things progressing?

steady – we simply can't tell. You couldn't have any confidence in any statement about any trend from the data shown in figure 8.3b.

Where does the noise shown in figure 8.3 come from? Well, temperatures can be looked upon as having 5 components – a trend, a seasonal variation, other cyclical variations, 'odd events' and random fluctuations. These are illustrated in figure 8.4.

Figure 8.4 The elements of global temperature time series

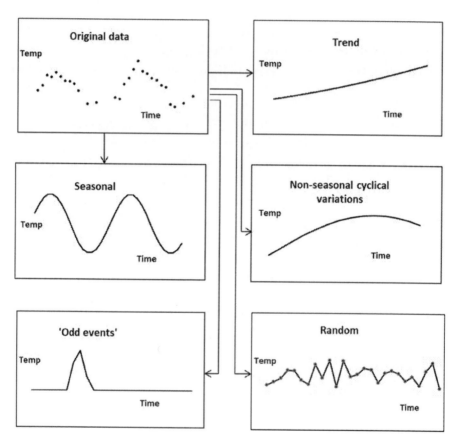

We would consider it crazy to compare a summer's day with a winter's day and on this basis claim that global temperatures are changing: it's obvious that the seasonal variations must be removed to get a good measure of any global warming. Potentially however, all the other components except the trend could be considered noise. If we left these components in the time series the chances of having any confidence in the value for the temperature trend would be very low. [Note that having a lot of noise is valuable to climate change deniers as they can say that it's impossible to determine whether the global temperature is rising or not].

But we don't have to work with so much noise since many of the components are known fairly accurately. One known non-seasonal cyclical variation is sunspot activity which has a fairly regular 11-year cycle whose effects on the weather are well known. Similarly, there are the El Nino events in the Pacific that occur at irregular intervals of two to seven years and last between 9 months and two years. We know when these events happened and climate scientists can estimate their effects. Odd events such as major volcanic eruptions can also be allowed for. So the effects of many of the non-trend components of global temperature can mostly be eliminated from a temperature time series. These eliminations will increase the signal-to-noise ratio - the noise now simply being a combination of the parts of the non-trend components that haven't been removed completely, the irreducible randomness in the weather and measurement error[9].

We now know where the noise comes from but how will it show itself? To better get a grip on this we now digress into coin tossing – please bear with me!

Coin tossing and apparent global warming

If you toss an unbiased coin you expect the coin to fall heads half the time and tails half the time – a 50% chance of either event (a probability of 0.5). The reason it's sometimes heads and sometimes tails is because of random factors in the coin toss – the way the coin is flipped, perhaps small amounts of air turbulence, the surface the coin falls on.

The probability of getting a head on the first toss is ½. This is also the probability of getting a head on the second toss. The chance of getting 2 heads is therefore ½*½ = ¼. For 2 tails it's the same. For one head and one tail it's ½, double the ¼ for heads and the ¼ for tails as the two results, T H and H T, are both one head and one tail outcomes. Note that the chance of getting any <u>specified</u> sequence is the same: for example, the sequence H H H H H is as equally likely to occur as H H T H T: the

Chapter 8 How are things progressing?

probability of getting each of these sequences is around 3% ($\frac{1}{2}*\frac{1}{2}*\frac{1}{2}*\frac{1}{2}*\frac{1}{2} = 0.03$).

If we did 100 tosses rather than just 5, then the chance of getting a sequence of 5 heads somewhere in the series will increase considerably. If we had 200 tosses the chance of getting a run of 5 heads would further increase. Crucially, if a large dataset is assembled not only can such a run happen <u>it's almost inevitable that it will</u>[10].

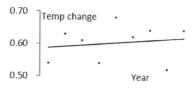

Figure 8.5a 2002-2009

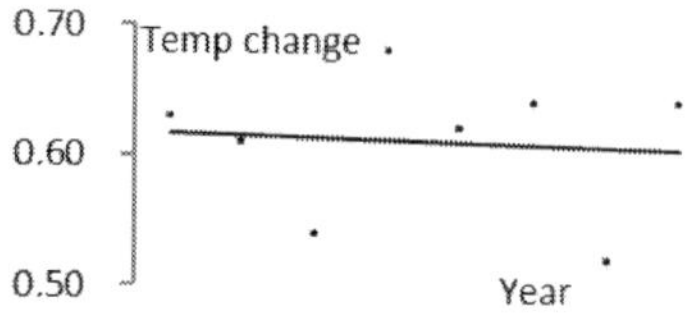

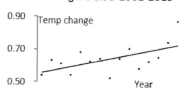

Figure 8.5b 2001-2009

If we simplify things in the temperature time series and crudely label temperatures above the trend line as *positive* and those below the trend line as *negative*, then we can view the noise in a set of temperatures as similar to the tossing of a coin. The probability of getting 5 below-average values in a sequence of 5 temperature measurements is 3%.

Figure 8.5c 2001-2015

Let's look now at real global temperature data. The 3 graphs in figure 8.5 plot annual temperature changes, with the changes relative to the mean temperature over the period 1951-1980[11].

Consider figure 8.5a. This shows the temperatures for the period 2002-2009. This graph is composed of the trend and random fluctuations and is the sort used by climate change deniers to 'prove' that global temperatures are no longer rising - or indeed, even falling. The flatish trend line suggests that this might indeed be the case.

But note in figures 8.5b and c what happens as we simply add another data point (for 2001) and/or we extend the graph to include data to 2015.

Disinformation: identifying devious data and iffy information

One or two extra points significantly change the signal coming out of the data: the chosen start and end points do matter.

An overall drive in statistics - and stressed in much of this book – is to unearth valid signals by reducing the noise: by accounting for known factors and by increasing the sample size. In our discussion of global warming so far we have reduced the noise by removing known effects and in figure 8.5 tentatively looked at sample size. We now look more closely at the effect of increasing the sample size.

With a time series, increasing the sample size means increasing the time over which data is collected. So instead of taking periods between 2001 and 2015 as in figure 8.5 we can improve the chance of identifying any trend by using all the available data - as in figure 8.6. One lesson here is that there

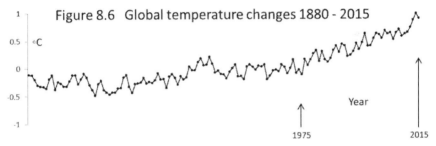

are quite a few time periods when there were 5 or more consecutive upward temperature changes, many where the local trend was flat and many where the trend was downwards. Indeed, over the first 4 decades or so at the start of the series the temperature trend was definitely downwards – global cooling apparently.

Figure 8.6 is probably the fullest picture of global surface temperatures it's possible to find. An interesting - and solid - finding is that the global surface temperature rise since 1975 has been 0.017°C per year, with the noise[9] being about 5 times larger.

Chapter 8 How are things progressing?

Key points

- Beware a single piece of data. A single piece of data gives no reference points to judge it by. If some obvious data points are excluded be very wary.
- Be suspicious if the obvious start or end dates aren't used but obscure ones are – or if no time frame is specified.
- If changing the start or end dates of a time series by a small amount makes a large change in an apparent trend then it's probably not a genuine trend at all.
- Smoothing a time series is a way of unearthing a trend, and it can be done through the use of moving averages. One characteristic of a moving average is that if the data has a periodic fluctuation such as the seasons, then applying an average of that period will eliminate that variation.
- A time series is bound to show sections that indicate a 'local' trend. Crucially, if a large enough dataset is assembled not only can such local trends occur it's almost inevitable that they will.

9 THE COMMENTARIAT AND ITS DATA SOURCES

Consider the credibility of your information sources. Most people will only access the news channels which most closely reflect their views. Thus the news items they read are unlikely to be challenging and many articles won't be read in sufficient detail to unearth inconsistencies or lack of evidence – and deviousness. So although it's unlikely that this chapter will alter your reading habits, the hope is that it may spark thoughts on how material can sensibly be assessed for veracity and credibility.

However, here's a challenge! Stop accessing your normal news outlet for a week, replacing it with its 'opposite number': The Daily Telegraph for The Guardian or vice-versa, BBC News for Sky News perhaps. Then for a week study news items in both outlets to the same depth. It can be very illuminating!

On Thursday 19th October 2017 Mrs May flew to Brussels to attend an EU Council Meeting. The main point on her agenda was the progress of the Brexit negotiations. The headlines from 5 UK media sources[1] about what happened are reproduced in textbox 9.1. Which one(s) are you inclined to believe, and why is this? Would your view change if you knew the author of the excerpts and/or the hosting media outlet?

Chapter 9 The commentariat and its data sources

> ### Textbox 9.1 Extracts from UK Media Outlets
>
> ***Brexit: Talk of deadlock is exaggerated, says Donald Tusk*** Reports of deadlock over Brexit negotiations may have been exaggerated, European Council President Donald Tusk has said after a Brussels summit. Progress was "not sufficient" to begin trade talks with the UK now but that "doesn't mean there is no progress at all", he said.
>
> ***Theresa May privately agrees to pay up to €40billion Brexit divorce*** Theresa May has privately assured European Union leaders that Britain will pay for current and future liabilities amounting to about €40billion, or $47billion. That figure, however, was dismissed this week by the president of the European Parliament, Antonio Tajani, as "peanuts".
>
> ***Theresa May begs EU leaders provide Brexit deal British public will accept*** Theresa May has pleaded with EU leaders to allow a Brexit deal which she can sell to British voters.
>
> ***£20bn? You're having a laugh!*** Theresa May shared an awkward joke with Angela Merkel and Emmanuel Macron. The talks have been locked in an acrimonious stalemate over EU demands for Britain to pay an exit bill some in Europe still believe should be £100billion - five times higher than the £20bn the UK has offered.
>
> ***Reasons to be cheerful*** Donald Tusk says EU will prepare to talk trade in December and blasts downbeat Brexit envoy after talks with 'optimistic and positive' Theresa May. And in a double boost for the Prime Minister the Commission President Jean Claude Juncker has said he DOES expect a deal between Britain and the EU to go ahead in the end.

   In the last two chapters the crucial need for context surrounding a news item has been highlighted. We now look at the wider context: - at the soundness of the source data that's being used and at the trustworthiness of the commentators who are using them.

Disinformation: identifying devious data and iffy information

The way in which we get information about things happening in the world isn't a clear-cut process. Figure 9.1 indicates the 4 major routes by which information reaches us.

Figure 9.1 Media data and information flows

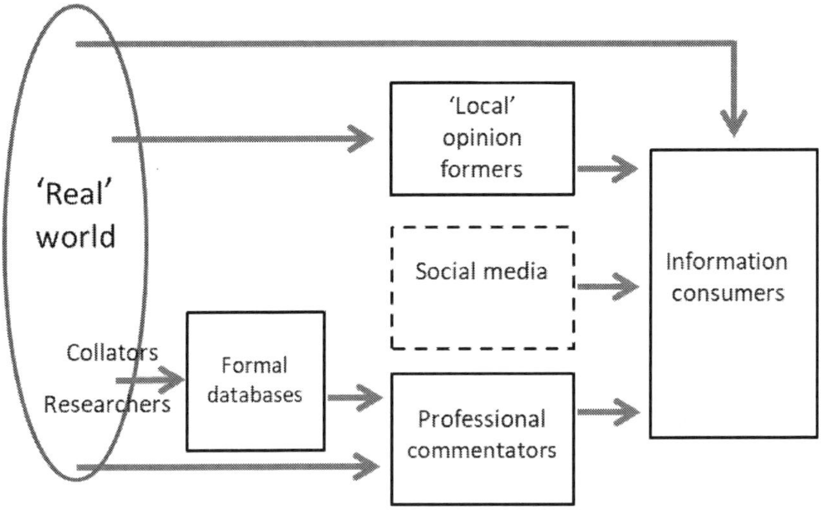

One route is through our own direct experience and observation of the real world. Another is via 'local' opinion formers – our family, friends and work colleagues. These links are generally face-to-face or directly via e-mail or phone. A third conduit for information is social media which <u>can</u> be informative but constitute something like the wild west of information. Conspiracy theories and fake news abound. In 2017 considerable concern was expressed about Russian 'troll factories' that had flooded the social media with false stories – allegedly to help the Trump campaign in the US and the Brexit campaign in the UK. The lack of any significant knowledge about the authors of many social media news items makes these items almost worthless. Even where the author is known, social media is suspect: who would bother with Trump's tweets if he wasn't POTUS? For these reasons social media will not be considered further. [It's important to note that this isn't to dismiss 'non-traditional' information outlets: blogs, podcasts and the like are increasing being used by professional commentators].

Chapter 9 The commentariat and its data sources

Important as these 3 paths can be, it's only the fourth route that we will be exploring here. This is what I have termed the formal route via professional commentators operating in the press, both print and internet, TV and radio – in short, the commentariat. These professional commentators are using formal databases[2] produced by official bodies and researchers as well as their experiences and observations of the real world. As we consider the producers of these databases and the professional commentariat I offer my view as to the worth of these sources. How will your ratings compare?

So far in this book the terms *data* and *information* have been used pretty much interchangeably but now a distinction now needs to be made. Data is the raw material for information, but on its own it's meaningless - it needs to be put into context. Putting it in context produces something worthwhile – it produces information. Blending this information with your own experience and expertise produces knowledge.

Assessing the trustworthiness of media outlets

Newspapers, TV, radio and the internet provide forums within which most columnists and pundits place their news items. These communication channels generally advocate the policies of the owner and/or editor, with the occasional guest contributor offering an 'opposition view'. So the first consideration when judging the credibility of a news item is to consider the provenance of the media outlet hosting it. Very significantly, who owns the outlet – a Trust, a single owner or a company? Who finances it and is that support disclosed?

There used to be a very sharp distinction between the (quality) broadsheet newspapers and the (more popular) tabloids. Even with the various other media and the size of the print editions themselves changing, this distinction - broadsheet and tabloid - can still be made for all news channels. One distinction is the balance between opinion and the underpinning facts and particularly the level of any personal abuse and emotion used to subvert counter arguments. This emotion can take many forms. Whilst it's quite in order for a commentator to be discounted because of past failures in their field – as will be shown later - it's quite

Disinformation: identifying devious data and iffy information

another to use emotion and personal abuse to attempt to weaken someone's case. This is put rather neatly in a letter to *The Guardian*[3] following the sad Charlie Gard case *While tabloid newspapers employ emotion applied to speculation, professionals employ reason applied to evidence.*

A significant feature that distinguishes a quality media outlet is its willingness to allow articles and letters to the editor that are contrary to the general tone and political tenor of the outlet. But you need to be watchful – some newspapers carry the odd dissenting letter chosen because it's such a poor letter.

My groupings of media outlets readily accessible in the UK are as follows:

- <u>Group 1 Broadsheet</u>: Bloomberg, The Daily Telegraph, The Financial Times, The Guardian, The i, The Independent, The Times and their Sunday editions, BBC News, Sky News, ITV News, Channel 4 News.

- <u>Group 2 Tabloid</u>: Al Jazeera, Buzzfeed, The Daily Mail, The Daily Express, The Mirror, Russia Today, The Sun.

Validity 6/10 for the broadsheets; 3/10 for the tabloids with The Daily Mail at 4

In mid-2018 the Oxford University's Reuters Institute for the Study of Journalism[4] published a report based on 2000 UK respondents about their consumption of digital news. They were asked the question *How trustworthy would you say news from the following brands is? Use the scale below, where 0 is 'not at all trustworthy' and 10 is 'completely trustworthy'.* The national broadcasters, which must abide by strict impartiality rules, were the most trusted outlets: the BBC scored 7.0; ITV News 6.8 and Channel 4 News 6.7. *The Times* had the highest brand trust score (6.4) of any newspaper or news website, ahead of *The Guardian* (6.2), *The Independent* (6.1) and *The Daily Telegraph* (6.0) There was a clear drop to the *Daily Mail* and *Buzzfeed* (both 4.6) and *The Sun* at 3.9.

Having given some consideration to the hosting channels let's now move on to discuss the constituents of the two major elements of figure 9.1

Chapter 9 The commentariat and its data sources

that concern us here: the producers of the formal databases and the commentariat.

Producers of Formal Databases

The producers of formal databases provide much of the data used by the commentariat and can usefully be divided into the collators and the researchers.

Collators

These are usually formally recognised bodies with a remit to produce data about the past – the growth of the economy over the last year, the number of children in school etc. They are often national government agencies: in the UK these would include the Office for National Statistics and government departments. International agencies such as The Organisation for Economic Co-operation and Development, the United Nations and the many EU bodies are also collating data.

$$Validity = 9/10$$

Researchers

Governmental organisations These could well have researchers working within the same organisations as the collators but with a remit to provide data about the future. The Bank of England would be in both camps as would the Office for Budget Responsibility. One problem here is that there can be the suspicion that these organisations aren't independent if they are an arm of government. The 'official' forecasts from the Treasury about the consequences of Brexit were seen by many as deliberately distorted to support the government's pro-Remain position.

$$Validity = 7/10 \text{ for UK government organisations}$$

Academic researchers Academics are generally steeped in the methodology of the academic field in which they work. The advantage of this is that the framework within which they conduct their research is one that has been tried and tested and is generally transparent. The research published in most academic journals is what's termed 'peer reviewed'. In this process a researcher puts forward their research findings to the editor of a journal together with a clear statement of how they have arrived at their results. The editor then selects experts in the field to review the paper and assess whether it should be published. Academic books and monographs are also often subject to such peer review. This peer review process isn't only validating the results: it's validating the process by which the results were obtained.

Academics are human, and one motivation in publishing is likely to be to enhance their professional standing and that of their university. It appears that this could go too far. A small group of young researchers in the UK joined together in 2017 to highlight the pressure they are under from their supervisors to produce 'sexed-up' versions of their research. They claim in their *Bullied into Bad Science* campaign[5] that the imperative to publish or die leads to a tide of rushed, exaggerated and downright false research. These claims are backed up by David Spiegelhalter, professor for the public understanding of risk at Cambridge University, who told the Royal Statistical Society in 2017[6] that most studies contained inflated claims. Inflating claims must be condemned, but it should be borne in mind that it's unlikely that any resulting distortions will be as significant as those from most other sources: after all, science and engineering have been outstandingly successful in advancing human knowledge due in major part to the methodologies adopted.

Textbox 9.2 Academic Indiscipline

…It is extraordinary that a study purporting to show that encouraging men to inset sex toys into their bottoms would make them less homophobic and transphobic was accepted by *Sexuality & Culture*. Moreover it was praised by a peer reviewer as an important contribution to science. A paper on 'Solidarity Feminism as an intersectional Reply to Neoliberal and Choice feminism" was accepted by *Affilia*, a leading feminist social work journal, even though it was largely a rewriting of a chapter of *Mein Kampf*….

But what of the social sciences? *The Times* reports[7] on hoax publications accepted for social science journals. An excerpt from its editorial is given in textbox 9.2. These are amusing cases but both the writing of such articles

Chapter 9 The commentariat and its data sources

and their acceptance puts a question mark over academic research in the social sciences.

Another worrying area is the source of funding for academics. In 2017 the US-based Campaign for Accountability[8] identified that Google had funded, directly or indirectly, 329 academic articles that support its positions. More than a quarter of those funded directly by Google didn't disclose the source of their money.

Validity = 8/10 for the physical sciences; 6/10 for the social sciences. Both heavily discounted if the source of funding isn't apparent.

Researchers in think tanks A think tank (alternatively called a policy institute or a research institute) is an organisation that performs research and advocacy on topics such as social policy and economics. They are mostly not-for-profit organisations. They employ a body of experts but, unlike in universities, these experts tend to be focussed on political or commercial goals. Their methodologies could be sound but often they aren't made public and thus the results may well be partial. Examples of think tanks in the UK are the Adam Smith Institute, whose main focus is the introduction of free market policies; the Centre for Social Justice, established to seek effective solutions to the poverty that blights parts of Britain; Chatham House, a centre for policy research on international affairs; and the Institute for Public Policy Research aiming to invigorate left wing thinking. These are very reputable think tanks, all considered 'highly transparent by the accountability group Transparify[9]. But overall, think tanks are of quite variable quality.

Some think tanks have been set up to achieve very narrow political goals. For example, The Global Warming Policy Foundation is a think tank in the UK whose stated aim is to challenge "extremely damaging and harmful policies" envisaged by governments to mitigate anthropogenic global warming. Because it operates a subsidiary as a charity, the GWPF isn't legally required to report its sources of funding and has declined to reveal them, citing privacy concerns. Perhaps it's funded by the oil companies! Think tanks have an axe to grind: if they hide the source of their funding and/or the methodology they have used, then the results they

Disinformation: identifying devious data and iffy information

publish should be viewed with great caution. Transparify judges GWPF to be 'highly opaque'.

The Institute for Economic Affairs is a thinktank which is often on the BBC and other TV channels espousing its causes. It's similarly rated by Transparify as 'highly opaque' as its funding isn't disclosed.

Validity = 6/10 - 9/10 where funding is acknowledged; otherwise 3/10

Researchers in commercial organisations Commercial researchers are working within companies that seek to make profits. Their work is subject to commercial confidentiality and the processes in their research are often not open to scrutiny. The way in which research is conducted in the pharmaceutical industry has been laid bare by Ben Goldacre in his book *Bad Pharma*[10]. For example, only the results of trials that support a drug are made public – those that fail to produce the results that are wanted are simply 'lost'. Recall that at the 95% confidence level one in 20 trials is likely to show an effect when the other 19 don't: if all you do is publish the one and keep quiet about the 19 you can trumpet a successful product.

Validity = 3/10

Responsible pollsters The pollsters considered here are those that have a national reputation: in the UK these would be organisations[11] such as ComRes, pollster for the BBC and The Independent; Ipsos MORI; YouGov; and Populus, the official pollster for The Times.

Validity = 8/10

Other providers of databases A vast number of people and organisations are providing data. These include the on-line polls described in Chapter 3, often carried out simply to generate headlines and nothing more, and charities which, although worthy, are unlikely to be carrying out the research in a valid way unless they devolve the survey to an authoritative third party. But to do valid research requires resources that charities often don't have. And charities have axes to grind and do do so.

Validity = very variable from 0/10 to 5/10

Chapter 9 The commentariat and its data sources

Before leaving this discussion around the production of formal databases it's interesting to note the findings of the Ipsos MORI Veracity poll[12]. In this poll, the trustworthiness of 24 professions was assessed with people being asked *Now I will read you a list of different types of people. For each would you tell me if you generally trust them to tell the truth, or not.* The top spot was held by nurses with a score of 94%: at the bottom were politicians with 17%. Of the professions likely to be in the forefront of producing databases the scores were doctors 91%, professors 85%, scientists 83% and civil servants 59%.

The Commentariat

Within the context of the host media channel, a primary consideration when assessing a news item is whether you know who the authors are. If no name appears be very wary. If authorship is acknowledged what do you know of the author(s)? What are their qualifications, experience and track record? Very significantly, who is supporting them financially and, just as significantly, is that support disclosed?

Politicians Politicians are both producers and consumers of information. As producers they find themselves in a very difficult position. UK Secretaries of State who are charged with formulating and implementing policy seldom have any significant expert knowledge in the areas they have responsibility for. For example, in 2017 Michael Gove was made Secretary of State for Environment, Food and Rural Affairs: one commentator said that in his adult life Gove had never been outside the M25. [This does him a slight injustice – until he went away to University he lived with his family who had a business servicing the fishing industry in Aberdeen]. This ignorance, coupled with cabinet responsibility, forces MPs into rather evasive and unfocussed utterances when asked to express opinions. MPs seldom tell downright untruths, but a lot of their skill does lie in obfuscation and deception.

Validity 3/10 when in government; 6/10 when in opposition

Columnist and pundits As well as expressing their own general views, columnist and pundits are converting the data in the formal databases into articles for their readers and listeners. How well are they doing this? Michael Gove's encouragement to ignore expert opinion in favour of simple assertion was mentioned in the Foreword. The author of textbox 6.1 (Dominic Raab) goes on from attacking the use of a couple of variables in one economic model to pour scorn on all the other economic models of the time. The two excerpts[13, 14] from the then Daily Mail columnist Melanie Phillips given in textbox 9.3 are similarly dismissive of experts and expert opinion.

> **Textbox 9.3 The Views of Melanie Phillips**
>
> A) The reason why so many scientists produce research purporting to demonstrate anthropogenic global warming is that grant-funding and academic advancement depend upon producing such a finding.
>
> B) It was Mr Wakefield who first made the devastating claim that the triple jab for measles, mumps and rubella can provoke both autism and bowel disease in a small proportion of children. The British and international medical authorities united to dismiss it, scorning his research as worthless and insisting the vaccination was perfectly safe.
> Report after report were published to rebut his findings, with MPs and ministers - including Prime Minister Tony Blair - joining the chorus that there was no cause for concern. According to Mr Wakefield, his life was made impossible. His funding started to dry up, professional collaborations were broken off, and researchers were allegedly bribed or threatened not to have anything to do with him.

There are profound lessons to learn from the way in which Gove, Phillips, Raab and many other commentators operate. They latch onto one or two perceived weaknesses in the methodology used to establish the databases and then use these apparent failures to discredit the model's predictions – perhaps the whole methodology and maybe the whole of the associated science. They engage in a most shallow way with the modelling/science because they know very little about it. Rather, they

Chapter 9 The commentariat and its data sources

attack the motives and/or the integrity of the modellers/experts and claim that modellers/experts are only saying what they are because it will enhance their careers and get research grants, or that they are lazy. I can accept that people operating outside of the accepted wisdom may not be getting a fair deal in terms of research grants. But this must be shown to be the case. For example, in the Wakefield case why did his funding start to dry up - were his research proposals scientifically valid? [Interestingly, Melanie Phillips is scathing about the methodology used by the overwhelming majority of climate scientist, but doesn't seem to have queried the methodology used by the lone Mr Wakefield].[15]

At least Raab made some effort to engage with the available databases. However, the editorial reproduced as textbox 7.2 illustrates the almost complete disregard that authors can show for the facts. As the copious endnotes of Chapter 7 show, there was a very large volume of data which the author could have accessed to develop a cogent argument and they chose not to. The moral here is to ask of a news item whether data sources are cited: this at least allows interested parties to look at the basic data.

This condemnation of how some politicians and commentators try to counter the findings of experts isn't a call to blindly accept what experts say – you should apply common sense to all pronouncements and reflect on context. The call is for scepticism not cynicism. If you are sceptical then see what other experts are saying. Only experts can expertly challenge experts, although if data sources are cited the enthused reader can generally make more sense of what they are reading.

Obviously it's rather difficult for people to challenge experts or even to understand what they are saying, as they are likely to use esoteric jargon. But there are experts who do put across their ideas in a form that can be interpreted by the non-expert: examples are Richard Dawkins on evolution and genetics, Ben Goldacre on the pharmaceutical industry, George Monbiot on environmental matters and David Spiegelhalter regarding risk.

Validity 3/10 for non-experts; 9/10 for experts discussing their field of expertise

It's now interesting to return to the Ipsos MORI Veracity Index and see what the public's scores were for members of the commentariat. Scientists scored 83%, local councillors 41%, business leaders 36%, journalists 27%, government ministers 19% and the generality of politicians 17%.

Other things to look out for in assessing the value of a news item

Absurd rubbishing links The extract in textbox 9.4 is from an article in the Daily Mail by James Delingpole[16] under the title *Colossal Con trick* He doesn't like wind turbine energy generation and starts his case by linking this distaste with the Nazis.

Textbox 9.4 Colossal Con Trick

The world's biggest wind turbine – nearly three times the height of Big Ben – is to be built off the North-East coast. But James Delingpole says the idea these giants will solve our energy problems is simply hot air.

What could be more clean and natural than harvesting energy from the power of wind using gigantic turbines? Environmentalists have dreamed of this since at least the Thirties, when a Nazi German inventor called Dr Franz Lawaszeck theorised how to solve his country's energy problems at a stroke.

He wrote: 'Wind power, using the cost-free wind, can be built on a large scale. Improved technology will, in the future, make it no more expensive than thermal power . . . the wind towers must be at least 100 metres high, the higher the better, ideally with rotors 100 metres in diameter.'

Wind power was all the rage among Nazis, many of whom shared the party's fanatical commitment to the environment. Other big fans included Hitler's favourite commando, Otto Skorzeny.

After an eventful war — which included springing Mussolini from his mountain-top jail in a daring glider operation and planning a (happily abortive) assassination attempt on Churchill, Roosevelt and Stalin — the plucky SS-Obersturmbannführer settled in Spain where he spent his later years campaigning on behalf of the nascent wind industry.

But it has taken until now for the Nazis' dream of a world powered by wind to become even remotely plausible.

Chapter 9 The commentariat and its data sources

Quotes from famous people Of particular concern is the practice of well-known people using their eminence in one field to 'lever up' their comments in another. Years ago the then world snooker champion Steve Davis was used as a cheer leader for the Conservative party with the slogan *Let's pot some reds*. In mid-2017 the world famous physicist Stephen Hawking inveighed against the policies of Jeremy Hunt[17] the long-serving Secretary of State for Health. Many people sided with Hawking, one person stating that they would trust a world-famous scientist rather than someone who had studied PPE at university! Hawking does have a severe disability that has required him to attend hospital very many times over many years, but the special insight Hawking had of the strategic issues in the Health Service wasn't clear.

The conduct of the former UK Chancellor of the Exchequer Nigel Lawson in the climate change debate is another example of someone expert in one field moving into another in which they are inexpert. His rhetoric has been described by climate scientists as ignorant and dangerous. Of late he seems to have acknowledged the science and is now focussing on the economic and political measures that can be taken to mitigate the effects of climate change. This is very welcome: he has shifted to an area where his expertise allows him to make a considerable contribution.

The main front-page headline in *The Guardian*[18] - *Brexit's the worst ever decision says Bloomberg* - used one man's opinion to dominate the news. Bloomberg is a very successful businessman and had a good record as mayor of New York, but where is his expertise in European affairs and with what led up to Brexit? When lecturing around the world on global health matters Rosling[19] reports on the massive ignorance experts in one field had in other – sometimes closely related – fields. For example, he recounts addressing a large group of young scientists and Nobel laureates in physiology and medicine. When asked to choose the number of 1-year old children who have been vaccinated against some disease, from the possible answers 20%, 50% and 80%, only 8% of the audience got the right answer (80%).

Martin Rees the astronomer royal in the UK notes a tendency for eminent scientists to lend their support to general issues. He is quoted as saying[20] of Nobel prize winners *Even the best scientists have narrow expertise, and their opinions on general topics carry no special weight. It is possible to find a laureate to support almost any cause, however eccentric, and some exploit their status.*

Simple little descriptors Obviously newspapers and other outlets rely heavily on information passed to them by people in the know – or who say they are in the know. In many case the information is given on the understanding that the sources remains anonymous. But take care when the source is described as a leading city economist, party grandee, esteemed backbencher, well-respected back bencher, a well-regarded source, a source with knowledge of…. These descriptors boost both the credibility of the information and the standing of the author, but who is to know whether the citation is apt and the quote accurate - or simply fabricated?

The issue of anonymous sources was highlighted in September 2018 when *The New York Times*[21] published blisteringly accusations against the President written by what it termed a 'Senior Administration Official'. The views expressed were explosive, partly because this official could have been anyone in the White House inner circle from the Vice President downwards. Or, as Trump himself maintained, the article could simply have been made up by someone on the newspaper's staff. My sympathies lie with Trump.

Vacuous phrases These are phrases that sound reasonable and perhaps even appear to mean something until you apply the age-old test *Would anyone say the opposite?* If they wouldn't, does the phrase mean much? Recent examples are:

- Brexit means Brexit - *Brexit doesn't mean Brexit*

- We are going to get the best deal for Britain - *We're not going to get the best deal for Britain* or *We're going to get the worst deal for Britain*

- I did what I thought was right – *I did what I thought was wrong*

- We need a balance between x and y. *We don't need a balance between x and y*

Chapter 9 The commentariat and its data sources

and my favourite, from a spokesperson for No.10[22]

- We are working to secure a good deal for Britain and also a good deal for the European Union. We think we are heading in the right direction and we're confident of achieving that.

    Any version along the lines of - *We are working to secure a bad deal for Britain and also a bad deal for the European Union. We think we are heading in the wrong direction and we're unsure of achieving that.*

Facts/reality Finally, two personal bugbears of mine to close on. First, the dreaded *I'm very clear…* or the even worse *Let me be clear…* followed by a self-satisfied pause denoting that the speaker is making only one thing clear – that any failure to understand is your fault – you, stupid, just shut up and pay attention.

Second, be wary when a statement is prefaced with any of the following:

The fact is…
The reality of the situation is ….
The reality is ….
Here's the truth…..

In very many cases what follows is an opinion – sometimes with no supporting evidence whatsoever. Here *alternative facts* don't even mean *selective facts* but simply *no facts*.

Key points

- The major formal avenue by which people can get valid information is through the commentariat – the authors of news items and their host organisations – and from the data sources they rely on.
- The background of the members of the commentariat and producers of these databases is a vital consideration in determining the credibility of the news item. Their reputations should be at stake. As should the host channel: would you rather read The Times, The Daily Telegraph or Pravda?
- If you want information that's generally reliable, expect to pay for it.
- Has the commentator cited their data sources? If not, be wary of the arguments they use.
- The questions to ask of any media article about a subject that you are very interested in are:
  - Where did the base data come from – a recognised university, a research institute or respected polling company?
  - Was the sample size appropriate and was there a control group?
  - Who funded the study? Is there any conflict of interest or bias?
  - Where was the article published – peer-reviewed academic paper, reputable newspaper, reputable social media outlet?
  - Was it an observational study, an experimental study or a review of a set of previous studies.

GLOSSARY

Academic researchers: staff members in a university who undertake research.

Arithmetic mean: the average that's normally abbreviated to 'the mean' – see below.

Association: a link between two or more variables.

Attribute: an element or characteristic of an individual.

Average: a measure around which the data in a dataset tend to cluster.

Bell curve: see Normal Distribution.

Bias: a systematic distortion introduced into a dataset or statistic due to the way in which the dataset has been derived.

Big data: a very large collection of data from many varied databases, typically terabytes in size or larger.

Brexit: British exit, the decision for the UK to leave the EU.

Causation: a linked set of events where one event gives rise to another.

Central Limit Theorem: the finding that (almost) whatever the distribution of values in a population, the means of samples drawn from the population are normally distributed – they follow the bell curve.

Collators: are formally recognised parties with a remit to produce, collect and combine data about the past.

Commentariat: the group of people in the news media who translate data into information for information consumers.

Confidence interval: the two values between which a population value can be expected to lie with a specified confidence level when the value has been estimated from a sample. It's the plus-or-minus figure usually reported in newspaper and television opinion polls. [Also known as the margin of error].

Disinformation: identifying devious data and iffy information

Confidence level: represents how often the true population mean lies within the confidence interval. It's expressed as a percentage.

Consumer Price Index (CPI): a measure of inflation used in the UK that reflects the change in prices of a typical basket of goods and services. It's more restrictive than the RPI as it doesn't include several important items such as housing costs. It takes into account the way in which one good or service can be substituted by another. The geometric mean is used in its calculation.

Continuous variable: a variable that can take on any value within a specified range.

Correlation: a relationship between the corresponding values of a pair of variables. Such a link doesn't mean that a change in one variable causes a change in the other variable.

Correlation coefficient: also known as Pearson's r, is a measure that quantifies the strength of a linear correlation.

Cum hoc ergo propter hoc: with this, therefore because of this. One of the common logical fallacies.

Data: quantitative measurements about people and things.

Database: a formal collection of datasets.

Dataset: a collection of numerical statements about an entity.

Descriptive statistics: measures that describe the features of a dataset.

Discrete variable: a variable that can only take on particular values. Very often the allowed values are integers.

Disinformation: verifiably false or misleading information which is created, presented and disseminated for economic gain or to intentionally deceive the public.

Distribution: the dispersion of the values in a dataset.

Entity: a single person/thing. A synonym of *Individual*.

Exponential: a change is considered to be exponential when the rate of change in a unit of time is proportional to the current value. For example, if there was growth in a population of 10% pa, then when the population is 1million the population would be 1.1million at the end of that year. When the population had grown to 2million the population would be 2.2million at the end of that year.

EU: the European Union.

Forecast: a prediction about the future.

Geometric mean: calculated by summing the reciprocals of data values

Glossary

and dividing this sum by the number of data values.

GDP: Gross Domestic Product, is a monetary measure of the market value of all the final goods and services produced – usually for a country and for a period of a quarter or a year.

IMF: International Monetary Fund.

Importance: not to be confused with significant when significance is used with a statistical meaning.

Imprecision: a measure of the random error in a piece of data or information.

Individual: in statistics, a single item of interest. A synonym of *Entity*.

Inexactitude: has two dimensions - imprecision and bias.

Inferential statistics: the method and techniques whereby population measures are deduced from sample measures; also the deduced measures themselves.

Information: data that's arranged to be of direct use.

Intelligence: the outcome of the meshing and reconciliation of sets of information.

Interquartile range: the difference between the lower and upper quartiles ie., the values that are respectively one quarter and three-quarters of the way along a ranked set of observations. It covers the 'middle half' of a ranked set.

Judgemental forecasting: predictions of the future based on the intelligence available to a group or an individual.

Linear: a relationship in which the effects are in constant proportion to the causes and where the effects of more than one factor acting at the same time are additive.

Margin of error: the two values between which a population value can be expected to lie with a specified confidence when the value has been estimated from a sample. It's the plus-or-minus figure usually reported in newspaper and television opinion polls. (Also known as the confidence interval).

Mathematical model: a simplified representation in which reality is represented by mathematical symbols and formulae. Such a description allows this version of reality to be explored by computer.

Mean: the value obtained by summing all the values in a dataset and dividing by the number of items in the set.

Median: the value such that 50% of values in the dataset are greater than or equal to it and 50% are less than or equal to it: It's the middle number in a ranked set of data.

Misinformation: information that's incorrect.

Mode: the most frequently occurring value in a dataset.

Model: a representation of reality, either one that already exists or a view of what might exist in the future.

Nominal scale: a scale of measurement in which items are differentiated one from another but no further distinction is made. It's used when grouping individuals.

Normal distribution: a bell-shaped curve describing the probability of occurrence of specified values of a variable.

OBR: the Office for Budget Responsibility is the official UK independent fiscal watchdog providing independent and authoritative analysis of the UK's public finances.

Observational Research: a type of research particularly prevalent in the social sciences and in marketing, involving the direct observation of people in their natural setting.

OECD: Organisation for Economic Co-operation and Development. It works with governments to understand what drives economic, social and environmental change.

OFSTED: the Office for Standards in Education, Children's Services and Skills. It inspects and regulates services that care for children and young people and services providing education and skills for learners of all ages.

ONS: Office for National Statistics, the recognised national statistical institute of the UK.

Ordinal scale: a scale of measurement that measures individuals according to the magnitude of an attribute. The higher the number assigned the more of the attribute the individual possesses. It's used when ranking individuals.

Policy institute: see Think tank.

Polling organisation: a professional body expert in surveying and interviewing.

Population: all the people/things about which there's a specific interest.

Population standard deviation: the standard deviation of individual values around the population mean.

Post hoc ergo propter hoc: after this, therefore because of this. One of the common logical fallacies.

POTUS: President of the United States.

Glossary

PPE: Philosophy, Politics and Economics.

Predictive analytics: the application of machine learning techniques to generate models for purposes of prediction.

Primary observer effect: inexactitude introduced by the person conducting the poll during the data gathering process.

Probability: the likelihood of an event/variable value occurring.

Probability distribution: a relationship describing the linkage between the chance of a specific value or a range of values occurring and that value or range of values.

Quantitative forecasting: represents a future situation in terms of mathematics so that predictions can readily be made.

Quartile: a 25% portion of a ranked set of values.

Quintile: a 20% portion of a ranked set of values.

Range: the 'distance' between the maximum and minimum values in a dataset.

Ratio scale: a scale of measurement where a difference in the amount of an attribute is represented by the same differences in measurement. It's used as a yardstick/ruler might be used.

Regression: the relationship between the values of one variable and those of another determined using least squares fitting procedures.

Regression to the mean: the act of going back to a previous state or the reversion to an average.

Research institute: see Think tank.

Researchers: include economists and scientists in governmental organisations, academics, investigators in think tanks, researchers in commercial organisations and responsible pollsters.

Retail Price Index (RPI): a measure of inflation used in the UK that reflects the change in prices of a typical basket of goods and services. The arithmetic mean is used in its calculation.

Sample: a subset of a population. The sample will contain individuals whose measured attributes will provide a dataset.

Sampling error: the result of using values in a sample to estimate the values for a whole population. As the sample is smaller than the population it cannot be completely representative of it.

Sample size: the number of individuals selected for measurement.

Sample standard deviation: the standard deviation of individuals in the sample around the sample mean.

Disinformation: identifying devious data and iffy information

Scale of measurement: the measuring tool by which an attribute of an individual is 'captured'.

Scenario: is a narrative providing an internally consistent view of how the future may plausibly turn out. It provides a context within which issues can be explored. It's not a forecast.

Secondary observer effect: the situation whereby a researcher imposes their own idiosyncrasies on already-collected data: consequently their findings might be inappropriately shaded.

Signal-to-noise ratio: the ratio of the size of a signal to the level of background noise.

Significance: shorthand for statistical significance. A result that's deemed significant is one that's unlikely to have occurred by chance: highly significant means the result is very unlikely to have occurred by chance.

Significance level: indicates how likely a pattern in a dataset is due to chance. The most common level used to indicate that something is good enough to be accepted is 95%. This means that the finding has a 95% chance of being true (and of course a 5% chance of being untrue).

Square root: is the value that when multiplied by itself gives the original value. Thus the square root of 25 (denoted by $\sqrt{25}$) is 5, since 5 * 5 = 25).

Standard deviation: is the square root of the variance.

Standard deviation of the sample means: the standard deviation of the means of many, same-sized samples around their overall mean.

Standardised normal distribution: a normal distribution with a mean of zero and a standard deviation equal to 1.

Statistics: a branch of mathematics dealing with the collection, analysis, interpretation, and presentation of numerical data.

Surrogate measure: a proxy or substitute quantity.

Tera: one million million: a thousand billion.

Think tank: alternatively called a policy institute or a research institute. An organisation that performs research and advocacy on topics such as social policy and economics.

Validity: an expression of the confidence in the veracity of a news item.

Variance: the average of the squares of the deviations of the individual data values from the mean of the dataset. All the squared values are added together and their mean is calculated. This mean squared deviation is termed the variance.

ENDNOTES

Foreword

1. Michael Gove: interview with Faisal Islam Sky News May 2016. [At a later date he claimed that he only meant economists].
2. Facts are old hat, Matthew Parris in his My Week column *The Times* 04/07/18.
3. Factfulness: ten reasons we're wrong about the world – and why things are better than you think, Hans Rosling (with Ola Rosling and Anna Rosling Ronnlund), *Sceptre* 2018.
4. President Trump has made 4,229 false or misleading claims in 558 days, Glenn Kessler, Salvador Rizzo and Meg Kelly, The Fact Checker, *The Washington Post* 01/08/2018.
5. EU Code of Practice on Disinformation, September 2018
6. Trump admits to having 'no idea' if U.S. had trade deficit with Canada *The Washington Post* 15/03/2018. [In fact, the U.S. has a trade surplus with Canada].
7. Tory minister Penny Mordaunt 'plain and simple lying' over Turkey joining EU, Andrew Marr show, BBC 22/05/2016.
8. A database of Factcheckers is maintained by Duke Reporters' Lab https://reporterslab.org/fact-checking/. Mark Stencel reports 156 Factcheckers are active in more than 50 countries 07/08/2018.
9. The politics of polling, Select Committee on Political Polling and Digital Media Report of Session 2017–19. Ordered to be printed 20 March 2018 and published 17 April 2018. HL Paper 106. Published by the Authority of the House of Lords.
10. All-party parliamentary group on literacy of the House of Commons, Lucy Powell MP, Chair, in her letter to The Guardian 13/06/18.

Disinformation: identifying devious data and iffy information

Introduction

Chapter 1 Summarising Datasets

1. How politicians poison statistics, Tim Hartford *The Financial Times,* 14/05/2016.
2. Statisticians more exactly term this mean the arithmetic mean. There are more esoteric versions of the mean.
3. *More or Less,* Radio 4, 25/08/2017. [This mistake later corrected by Tim Hartford, the presenter of *More or Less* 01/09/2017].
4. The calculations are based on the 9 lowest paid employees simply because of space limitations in the table.
5. The two sets of data have an even number of values. In such situations the middle value (the median) of each must be estimated as lying midway between the two values on either side of the middle.

Chapter 2 What's being reported?

1. How politicians poison statistics, Tim Hartford *The Financial Times* 14/05/2016.
2. 1995 the United Nations adopted two definitions of poverty, Wikipaedia.
3. OECD (2017), Poverty rate (indicator). doi: 10.1787/0fe1315d-en Accessed on 09/10/2017.
4. Child Poverty Act 2010. And http://researchbriefings.parliament.uk/ ResearchBriefing/ Summary/ SN07096. This Act was scrapped in 2016 in England (but not for the rest of the UK) and as at 2018 there are no official poverty measures for England.
5. UK Poverty 2017, *The Joseph Rowntree Foundation* 2017.
6. A new measure of poverty for the UK: a report by the Social Metrics Commission chaired by Philippa Stroud, Legatum Institute September 2018.
7. The cost of a child in 2018, Donald Hirsch, Child Poverty Action Group August 2018.
8. Greece's debts are not the problem, it is the state's inability to reform, Simon Nixon *The Times* 30/08/2018.

Endnotes

9. Caricaturing Labour and Tory economic policies is an insult to our intelligence, Ben Chu *The Independent* 04/10/2017.
10. *More or Less,* Radio 4 presented by Tim Hartford 15/09/2017.
11. The British Isles consists of the islands of Great Britain, Ireland and over six thousand smaller islands.
12. NHS is beyond fixing *Daily Telegraph editorial* 28/10/2017.
13. Budget boost for Hammond as deficit tumbles by £700m, Tom Knowles, *The Times* 21/10/17.
14. Surprise growth in economy set to bring interest rate rise, Philip Aldrick *The Times* 26/10/2017.
15. Productivity demons in our flawed economy are coming home to roost, Philip Aldrick *The Times* 21/10/2017.
16. RPI vs CPI: seconds out, round two, Nigel Hawkes, Full Fact Straight Statistics 31/08/2010 and The difference between CPI and RPI inflation – and why it matters, Merryn Somerset Webb *MoneyWeek* 18/08/2011.
17. The RPI is an arithmetic mean – ie, the prices of everything to be included in it are simply added up and divided by the number of items. The CPI is a geometric mean, calculated by multiplying the prices of all the items together and then taking the nth root of them, where 'n' is the number of items involved.
18. Note that in the view of the Royal Statistical Society the continued use of RPI for price and tax setting purposes is unwarranted as the measure is technically flawed. In 2012 the RPI was stripped of official 'national statistic' status.
19. Grayling says rail price hikes can be curbed if unions do same for pay, Gwyn Topham *The Guardian* 15/08/2018.
20. Bad news, Europhiles: things are looking up for business in Britain, Dominic Lawson *The Sunday Times* (Scottish edition) 20/08/2017.
21. The Returns to Higher Education Qualifications, BIS Research Paper Number 45 June 2011. Graduates earn £500,000 more than non-graduates, Elizabeth Anderson *The Daily Telegraph* 03/10/2017.
22. Two-speed Europe is here, and we're in the slow lane, Richard Partington *The Guardian* 04/09/2017.
23. Only reports relating to the whole of the UK have been included: regional reports, opinion pieces and forecasts have been ignored.

Chapter 3 Sampling

1. Office of National Statistics 2017.
2. Referendum on the United Kingdom's membership of the European Union Advice of the Electoral Commission on the referendum question included in the European Union (Referendum) Bill September 2015.
3. Let's be honest about the cost of immigration curbs, James Kirkup, Director of the Social Market Foundation *The Times* 06/06/2017.
4. Article by Rob Merrick *The Independent* 11/06/2017.
5. Boris would be a fool to think he's on top, Matthew Parris *The Times* 04/08/2018.
6. A concept and measurement of violence against women and men, Professor Silvia Walby, Lancaster University on *More or Less,* Radio 4, 29/09/2107.

Chapter 4 Statistics about Populations

1. Jenni Ervasti, Mika Kivimäki, Jenny Head, Marcel Goldberg, Guillaume Airagnes, Jaana Pentti, Tuula Oksanen, Paula Salo, Sakari Suominen, Markus Jokela, Jussi Vahtera, Marie Zins, Marianna Virtanen. Sickness absence diagnoses among abstainers, low-risk drinkers and at-risk drinkers: consideration of the U-shaped association between alcohol use and sickness absence in four cohort studies. Addiction, 2018; DOI: 10.1111/add.14249 also Teetotallers 'take more sick days than light drinkers' Alex Matthews-King *The Independent* 06/06/2018.
2. For more on the central limit theorem see Sampling Distribution of the Mean, David M. Lane Onlinestatbook.com or any other basic statistics book.
3. On Wikipedia you can see an animation of how spreads narrow as the size of the samples increases.
4. OFSTED Inspection report: Learndirect Ltd 20–23 March 2017.
5. Adult learning company faces collapse after trying to supress Ofsted report, Greg Hurst, *The Times* 15/08/2017.
6. And we've become more cheery since Brexit vote *The Daily Mail* 27/09/2017.
7. Throughout the discussion of voting we have considered simple yes/no voting choices, with outcomes that are roughly 50/50. If events were

nearer 0/100 then the margins of error will not be as accurately assessed. However, very many choices are binary and any result with close to 100% voting one way is almost certainly rigged, the vote is therefore unimportant and any inaccuracies in measurement immaterial.
8. For the trial of the weight loss drug to have a high level of validity there was a need to eliminate environmental factors as far as possible. Pollsters seek the opposite as they want any environmental effects – such as a change in voter sentiment – to be picked up across the whole sample.

Chapter 5 Association, Regression, Correlation and Causation

1. The 'distance' of the points from the line used in regression analysis is the variance.
2. See for example, Statistics For Dummies, 2nd edition, Deborah J. Rumsey *John Wiley and Sons Ltd* July 2016.
3. John Kampfner, CEO Creative Industries Federation – based on the article Arts foster scientific success: Avocations of Nobel, national academy, royal society, and sigma xi members, Letters to the Editor *The Times* 23/08/2017.
4. Are we overestimating the beneficial effects of alcohol in later life? The sick quitter and sick non-starter hypotheses Linda Ng Fat, Society for the Study of Addiction conference 2018.
5. Sick Britons find religion in God's waiting room Kaya Burgess, *The Times* 17/09/2018. Mature beliefs, Professor the Rev David Martin *The Times letters* 18/09/2018.
6. The secret of great Sats result? Extra music, and lots of it, Josh Halliday *The Guardian* 03/09/2017.
7. More school PE would boost children's brain power on top of physical fitness, says study, Sarah Knapton *The Daily Telegraph* 25/11/2017.
8. Common painkillers may raise risk of heart attack, Haroon Siddique *The Guardian* 10/05/2017.
9. History teaches you how to run the country, Mark Bailey *The Times* 11/08/2017. [In a letter to the Guardian on the 28/04/2018 David Head counters a previous author's antipathy to medieval studies by citing Carly Fiorina who was CEO of Hewlett Packard for several years as an industrial leader who has a degree in philosophy and medieval

history. I'm tempted to ask *What is it about historians and anecdotal evidence?* but then I realised that I was falling into the same trap as Messieurs Bailey and Head].
10. Hawthorne effect, Wikipedia.
11. The use of the word *regression* here means the act of going back to a previous state or the reversion to the average.

Chapter 6 Forecasting and Scenarios

1. World population estimates from 1800 to 2100: based on US Census Bureau historical estimates and the 'high', 'medium' and 'low' United Nations' projections made in 2010.
2. E-mail from the Office of Budget Responsibility regarding the number of variables in the OBR's macro-economic model 03/09/2017.
3. Brexit doom-mongers are using flawed forecasts to talk us down, Dominic Raab *The Daily Telegraph* 29/11/2016.
4. Transformation, Pascale, R.T., BBC Enterprises video 1994; Using scenarios to identify, analyze and manage uncertainty, Marsh, B in Chapter 3 of Learning from the Future: Competitive Foresight Scenarios, Fahey, L and Randall R.M. (eds) John Wiley 1998.
5. Delphi Technique a Step-by-Step Guide - Project Smart, Duncan Haughey   https://www.projectsmart.co.uk/delphi-technique-a-step-by-step-guide.php.
6. Dominic Raab *The Sunday Times* 26/08/2018.
7. Johnson wants to push May out, but it's too late now, John Rentoul *The Independent* 01/10/17.
8. Labour preparing for run on the pound, admits Corbyn, Francis Elliott, Sam Coates, Lucy Fisher *The Times* 27/09/2017.
9. Theresa May, Hansard 11/10/2017.
10. German army plans for EU collapse, David Charter *The Times* 07/11/2017.

Chapter 7 How do Things Compare?

1. In the autumn of 2017 an Office for National Statistics report listed the number of reported cases of crime in England and Wales (not the UK) and the total was indeed around 5million. However, this was <u>all recorded crime</u>. The number of murders recorded was around 700 and

Endnotes

the number of rapes was around 40,000, Statistical Bulletin:- Crime in England and Wales: year ending December 2017, www.ons.gov.uk.
2. History teaches you how to run the country, Mark Bailey *The Times* 11/08/17. [PPE is short for Philosophy, Politics and Economics].
3. Sexual harassment 'at epidemic levels' in UK universities, David Batty, Sally Weale and Caroline Bannock *The Guardian* 05/03/2017.
4. Still Just a Bit of Banter? Sexual harassment in the workplace in 2016, TUC report 10/08/2016.
5. The NHS is beyond fixing *Telegraph View* 28/10/2017 also *The Daily Telegraph* editorial 28/10/2017.
6. Mirror, Mirror 2017 International Comparison Reflects Flaws and Opportunities for better US Health care, 14/07/2017 and the 2014 update: How the U.S. Health Care System Compares Internationally 16/10/2014 The Commonwealth Fund.
7. Jeremy Warner *The Daily Telegraph* 22/10/2015.
8. Data used when discussing the state of the NHS.

1	2	3	4	5	6	7
	GDP	Pop	GDP/cap	% of GDP	US$	
France	2.5	67	42	11.1	4,660	12
Germany	3.5	82	48	11.2	5,380	29
Singapore	0.5	6	88			
Switzerland	0.7	6	60	12.1	7,260	75
UK	2.6	66	42	9.9	4,160	0
USA	18.5	326	57	16.9	9,630	132

Column 2 US$ Trillion IMF 2016   Column 3 Population in millions 2016
Column 4 US$'000 IMF 2016 with GDP measured in purchasing power parity
Column 5 % of GDP spent on health OECD 2015
Column 6 Spend per capita on health in US$ Column 7 % spend more than UK

[Note that it's difficult to compare the UK's health system with that of Singapore as the whole setup there is so different. However, Singapore's per capita GDP is around twice that of the UK.]

9. International comparisons of productivity, Office for National Statistics 06/10/2017.
10. Provision publication of Never Events reported as occurring between 1 April 2016 and 30 January 2017 27/02/2017.
11. Surgery and the NHS in numbers, Royal College of Surgeons 2017.

Disinformation: identifying devious data and iffy information

12. European health report 2018: More than numbers - evidence for all (2018) *www.euro.who.int/en/publications/abstracts/european-health-report-2018.-more-than-numbers-evidence-for-all-2018.*
13. Common painkillers may raise risk of heart attack, Haroon Siddique *The Guardian* 10/05/2017.
14. Alcohol use and burden for 195 countries and territories 1990-2016: a systematic analysis for the Global Burden of Disease Study 2016 GBD 2016 Collaborators *The Lancet* 23/08/2018.
15. Factfulness: Ten Reasons We're Wrong About The World - And Why Things Are Better Than You Think 03/04/2018y Hans Rosling with and Ola Rosling , Ola Rosling, Anna Rosling Rönnlund *Sceptre* 25/01/2018.
16. The answers to the *Little Quiz* are:

A	£2,000billion US$2.5trillion	B	65million
C	£35billion	D	0.5%
E	5%	F	£150billion
G	£100billion	H	£10%
I	5million	J	450million
K	Around half the size	L	almost halved
M	70 years	N	80%
O	Between 10 and 11billion		
P	1billion in the Americas, 1billion in Africa (1billion in N Europe and 4billion in Asia)		

Chapter 8 How are Things Progressing?

1. State of the Union Address, President Trump 30/01/2018. A State of the Union Address is given every year on the anniversary of a president's inauguration.
2. The president exaggerates his accomplishments in his address to Congress, Eugene Kiely, Brooks Jackson, Lori Robertson, Robert Farley, D'Angelo Gore, Vanessa Schipani and Saranac Hale Spencer *www.factcheck.org* Posted on 31/01/2018.
3. At the time of the Address only 11 months data was available for Trump's first year. The figures from the Obama era show conclusively

that job creation had started after the recession in 2008-9 and continued at as high or higher level than in Trump's first year.
4. Education secretary rebuked for misusing data, Rosemary Bennett, *The Times* 09/10/2018 and Education department's use of figures prompts 'serious concerns' from UK statistics watchdog, Benjamin Kentish *The Independent* 08/10/2018.
5. UK Economic Accounts time series dataset (UKEA) Series ID: IHYR Release date: 29 March 2018, Q on Q growth and annual.
6. Failures give room for success – Growing pains, Patrick Hosking, *The Times* 11/08/2018.
7. The growth in GDP can be influenced by many factors: for example, the buoyancy of foreign markets, changes in productivity and as mentioned in chapter 2, the change in the size of the working population. So it wouldn't be expected that the change in GDP would be anything like linear.
8. Global warming is the rate at which the global temperature is increasing, whilst climate change is also concerned with factors other than temperature, such as whether rainfalls are becoming heavier and wind speeds are changing.
9. Noise is the standard deviation of what remains unexplained 'around' the trend.
10. I'm indebted to *NOISE Lies, Damned Lies, and Denial of Global Warming* by Grant Foster 2010 *www.lulu.com* for this observation.
11. NASA GISS data, Goddard Space Flight Center, Sciences and Exploration Directorate, Earth Sciences Division, Global Annual Mean Surface Air Temperature Change 1880 to present, with the base period 1951-1980. *https://data.giss.nasa.gov/gistemp/graphs_v3/*.

Chapter 9 The Commentariat and its Data Sources

1. In order, these excerpts are from: *BBC News, Business Insider, The Metro, The Mail On-line* and *The Sun*.
2. Up to now the term dataset has been used. Now we use the term database which is a base of data encompassing many datasets.
3. Charlie Gard's sad fate, Dr Allan Dodds *The Guardian* letters 07/08/2017.

4. Which Brands do we Trust and Why? Posted by Antonis Kalogeropoulos *Digital News Report 2018* Reuters Institute for the Study of Journalism, Oxford University 2018.
5. Academics strike back against bad science, Bullied into Bad Science *The Times* 01/07/2017.
6. Trust in numbers, David Spiegelhalter, RSS President's Address 28/06/2017.
7. Academic Indiscipline Hoax publications have exposed a grievance culture that is poising social sciences *The Times editorial* 04/10/2018.
8. New Report Reveals Google's Extensive Financial Support for Academia, Campaign for Accountability 11/07/2017, and Silicon Valley's influence on thinktanks endangers democracy, Campaign for Accountability *The Guardian* 02/09/2017.
9. Think Tanks in the UK 2017: Transparency, Lobbying and Fake News in Brexit Britain, Transparify Bristol UK 08/02/2017. How Has Think Tank Transparency Evolved in 2018? Transparify Tbilisi, Georgia 17/07/2018.
10. Bad Pharma How drug companies mislead doctors and harm patients, Ben Goldacre, Fourth Estate, London 2012.
11. Polling companies as at mid-2018.
12. Veracity Index 2017 – all professions overview, Gideon Skinner and Michael Clemence, Ipsos MORI 26/10/2017.
13. http://www.melaniephillips.com/blow-science-sovereignty-sanity/6th June 2017.
14. MMR - The Truth Melanie Phillips *The Daily Mail*. Her work fully repudiated by BMJ. 2005 Nov 12; 331(7525): 1148.
15. Professor Malcolm Hill, private communication 2018.
16. Colossal Con Trick, James Delingpole *The Daily Mail* 26/04/2018.
17. Steven Hawking and Jeremy Hunt 'debate' *The Observer* 20/08/2017; *The Guardian* 26/08/17; *The Sunday Telegraph* 27/08/2017.
18. Michael Bloomberg: Brexit is 'stupidest thing any country has ever done' www.politico.eu 26 Oct 2017.
19. Factfulness: ten reasons we're wrong about the world – and why things are better than you think, Hans Rosling (with Ola Rosling and Anna Rosling Ronnlund) *Sceptre* 2018.
20. How myth of the lone Nobel-prize genius fails modern science, Robin McKie *The Observer* 30/09/2018.

Endnotes

21. The Quiet Resistance Inside the Trump Administration, Senior Administration Official *The New York Times* 05/09/2018.
22. Despicable' MP slammed after telling investors to avoid the UK, Jessica Elgot *The Guardian* 14/11/2017.

Printed in Poland
by Amazon Fulfillment
Poland Sp. z o.o., Wrocław